La Défense

Parc Monceau

18

Moulin Rouge

Bois de Boulogne

17

Opéra

Arc de
Triomphe

9

Concorde

8

Les Tuileries

Le Louvre

Trocadéro

1

7

Orsay

Les Invalides

16

6

Roland
Garros

Tour Eiffel

Montparnasse

15

14

Parc des expositions

Château de Versailles
30 km

Parc
Montsouris

Montmartre

La Villette

19

Sacré-Cœur

Buttes Chaumont

METRO

re du
ord

10

République

Père Lachaise

3 Le Marais

20

4

11

Notre-Dame

Disneyland
35 km

5

Bastille

Luxembourg

Nation

12

Bercy

nthéon

13

Grande Bibliothèque

Bois de Vincennes

Project Editor: Agnès Saint-Laurent
Art Director and Designer: Josée Amyotte
Graphic Designer: Chantal Landry
Image Processor: Johanne Lemay
Paris Arrondissement Maps: © www.comersis.com—
Cartography and Geomatics
Infographic Artist: Maryse Doray
Translators: Louisa Sage, Caitlin Stall-Paquet
Reviser: Robert Ronald
Proofreader: Elizabeth Lewis

Photographers: Judith Ritchie, except Reason 275:
Marie Forestier; and reasons 295, 296, 297 and 298:
Guillaume Fin
Illustrator: Gigi Mind

EXCLUSIVE DISTRIBUTOR:

For Canada and the United States:
Simon & Schuster Canada
166 King Street East, Suite 300
Toronto, ON M5A 1J3
phone: (647) 427-8882
          1-800-387-0446
Fax: (647) 430-9446
simonandschuster.ca

Catalogue data available from Bibliothèque
et Archives nationales du Québec

WARNING

As a city thirsty for new trends, Paris is constantly
changing, which means that the lifespan of bars,
restaurants and hotels varies greatly. Right up until
this book went to print, I walked through the city's
neighborhoods time and time again to ensure that
the information was up to date. However, as nothing
is safe from the passing of time, know that some
establishments might have moved or shut down
when you'll be visiting New York. Menus, prices,
fees and business hours are provided as a guideline
and are also subject to change. Enjoy your stay!

11-16

© 2016, Juniper Publishing,
division of the Sogides Group Inc.,
a subsidiary of Québecor Média Inc.
(Montreal, Quebec)

Printed in Canada
All rights reserved

Legal deposit: 2016
National Library of Québec
National Library of Canada

ISBN 978-1-988002-33-0

Conseil des Arts   Canada Council
du Canada   for the Arts

We gratefully acknowledge the support of the Canada
Council for the Arts for its publishing program.

We acknowledge the financial support of the
Government of Canada through the Canada Book Fund
for our publishing activities.

JUDITH RITCHIE

300

Reasons to Love

Paris

Table of Contents

Preface **9**
My Paris **11**

My Top Picks **12**

The Heart of Paris **19**
1st and 2nd Arrondissements

Upper Marais and Avant-Garde Fashion **63**
3rd and 4th Arrondissements

The Panthéon and Paris Chinatown **87**
5th and 13th Arrondissements

Saint-Germain and Surrounding Area **103**
6th and 14th Arrondissements

In the Shadow of the Eiffel Tower **127**
7th and 15th Arrondissements

The Chic Neighborhoods...................................147
8th and 16th Arrondissements

SoPi and Canal Saint-Martin.................177
9th and 10th Arrondissements

Bustling and Vibrant...............199
11th and 12th Arrondissements

Montmartre and Batignolles......................221
17th and 18th Arrondissements

Belleville and its Magical Vistas.....................247
19th and 20th Arrondissements

Paris Countryside..................267
Daytime Getaways

Index...................281
Acknowledgments...................287

Preface

It is a great pleasure to introduce 300 Reasons to Love Paris, the second in a series that began when I penned 300 Reasons to Love New York. When I threw myself into writing my first book, I had no idea that it would give birth to a series, and that the City of Light would be the second destination. It turned out to be a happy coincidence, because before moving to New York, I lived in Paris for almost two years. It is a beautiful and fascinating city, but I also found it intimidating and never really felt at home there. Every day had its share of mishaps, because I didn't know the codes: Paris can be a very closed city if you don't know the right people. In short, my experience was the opposite of Judith Ritchie's—Paris fits her like a glove. How I would love to have had her as my guide...

I admire her determination. In 2009, working as a journalist, she resolved to go and live in Paris. A year later, she arrived at Charles-de-Gaulle Airport with three suitcases in hand and no real plan. Two months after that, she got a prestigious job as beauty editor at the magazine L'Officiel de la Mode et de la Couture. The city's doors opened up to her. "Suddenly I found myself in an influential job, I had to be ahead of all the trends, but inside I felt more like a Parisian understudy. I had three months to prove myself," she said.

Judith plunged headfirst into the dynamism of Paris, forged an impressive network of contacts, and collected hundreds of addresses of interesting places to go, which—happily for the rest of us—she is now sharing here. A true lover of Paris, Judith knows the city's streets by heart. She adores the city's sophistication, the elegance of the women—young and old—peoples' courtesy, the pervasive appreciation of quality, the specialty shops, the Parisian art of savoring life.

When traveling, we are drawn to famous monuments and tourist sites, but we also want to delve deeper—to discover local treasures. When in Paris, we want to do as the Parisians do. In this personalized guide, Judith Ritchie tells us how. She helps us to discover a Paris that is luminous and colorful. She uncovers a city that reflects global trends while remaining profoundly traditional.

From small independent shops with rare finds, to cafeterias and gourmet restaurants, Judith Ritchie leads us into up-and-coming neighborhoods, over the most beautiful bridges, and down charming streets off the beaten path. This book has something for everyone: Parisians looking to rediscover their city, young hip explorers, and anyone who wants to see Paris in a new light.

Marie-Joëlle Parent
Author of 300 Reasons to Love New York and 300 Reasons to Love San Francisco.

The measure of love is to love without measure.

Saint Augustine

My Paris

I t was my work as a journalist that first introduced me to Paris in 2004, to cover the launch of a Guerlain perfume. Contrary to what you might think, I didn't fall in love at first sight. Initially I didn't understand the city, its streets radiating from the city center, its frantic pace, and its somehow warm aloofness. I returned several times, always for work: short, idyllic trips that were still rather "touristic." I circulated around Paris without ever truly experiencing its mysterious light. It wasn't until 2007, when I met and became friends with Romano Ricci, great-grandson of Nina Ricci and the perfumer who created Juliette has a Gun, that I discovered another Paris—the essential Paris known only to a handful of insiders. What did Parisians do morning, noon, evening and night? What were their points of reference, habits and well-kept secrets? My "initiation" into this realm was what awakened my passion for the city—the first flush of what has become a long love affair with the City of Light.

I left Montreal for Paris in 2009, on my 29th birthday, after completing my contract as beauty editor for *ELLE Québec*. Three suitcases in hand, a head full of dreams, and a rock-solid CV in my pocket. After all, what else did I need? I had Paris. Paris, my one true love!

I got a job as Beauty Editor at the magazine *L'Officiel de la Mode et de la Couture*—an incredible opportunity! I held that job for five years, in addition to blogging for the magazine Be, and appearing on the Direct 8 television show Mon Bien-Être. Through these professional experiences I became more "Parisian" than Parisians. Not only did I have to learn the essentials and basic values, but I also had to rise above that and imagine innovative trends in this exuberant city.

Energy, excitement, restlessness, agitation: Paris is a crucible of creativity, style, wordplay, wit, seduction, madness—and human connections. If Parisians know how to party, converse, socialize, enfranchise themselves, provoke and delight, they also know how to reinvent themselves. The proof is that the city's arrondissements are in constant evolution. Of course the heart of the city remains, with its fabulous monuments, age-old streets and alleys, the Louvre, the Grand Palais, the quays of the Seine, Notre-Dame-de-Paris—the essence of Paris and its charm. But if you dig a little deeper, and look to the Paris of the future, your heightened awareness will lead you to other neighborhoods, like the 19th and 20th arrondissements, which are perhaps less sexy at first glance, but oh so full of verve and home to many eccentric bourgeois-bohos (bobos, they say in Paris) who exemplify freedom of thought. Let's call it Grand Paris—a city that derives its equilibrium from the rich alchemy of social variety and cosmopolitan trade.

Whether you are new to Paris, an apprentice there, or a seasoned connoisseur, my "best of" guide will introduce you to a variety of restaurants—because Parisians are all foodies—beautiful walks and beautiful friends.

Without further ado, here are my 300 Reasons to Love Paris. Too few? Just enough? Too many? You be the judge! And when you're ready, come up with your very own reasons to love Paris.

Judith Ritchie

My TOP PICKS

NEO-BISTROS
Racines 2, 39 rue de l'Arbre-Sec, 1st (REASON 22)
SŌMA, 13 rue de Saintonge, 3rd (REASON 49)
L'Avant Comptoir, 9 Carrefour de l'Odéon, 6th (REASON 107)
Freddy's, 54 rue de Seine, 6th (REASON 107)
L'Ami Jean, 27 rue Malar, 7th (REASON 137)
52, 52 rue du Faubourg Saint-Denis, 10th (REASON 202)
Aux Deux Amis, 45 rue Oberkampf, 11th (REASON 220)
Septime, 80 rue de Charonne, 11th (REASON 226)
6 Paul Bert, 6 rue Paul Bert, 11th (REASON 232)
Au Passage, 1 bis Passage Saint-Sébastien, 11th (REASON 235)

STYLISH HOTELS
Hôtel Bachaumont, 18 rue Bachaumont, 2nd (REASON 29)
Buddha-Bar Hotel, 4 rue d'Anjou, 8th (REASON 155)
La Réserve, 42 Avenue Gabriel, 8th (REASON 158)
Hôtel Grand Amour, 18 rue de la Fidélité, 10th (REASON 203)
Hôtel Providence, 90 rue René Boulanger, 10th (REASON 209)

BRUNCH
Le Pain Quotidien, 5 rue des Petits Champs, 1st (REASON 18)
Claus, 14 rue Jean-Jacques Rousseau, 1st (REASON 21)
Baguett's Café, 33 rue de Richelieu, 1st (REASON 42)
Benedict, 19 rue Sainte-Croix-de-la-Bretonnerie, 4th (REASON 68)
Rachel's, 25 rue du Pont aux Choux, 3rd (REASON 68)

HAPPY HOUR / COCKTAILS / BARS
Garde-Robe, 41 rue de l'Arbre-Sec, 1st (REASON 22)
Coinstot Vino, 26 bis Passage des Panoramas, 2nd (REASON 27)
Experimental Cocktail Club, 37 rue Saint-Sauveur, 2nd (REASON 31)
Frenchie Wine Bar, 6 rue du Nil, 2nd (REASON 33)
Silencio, 142 rue Montmartre, 2nd (REASON 36)
Candelaria, 52 rue de Saintonge, 3rd (REASON 49)
Nüba, 34 quai d'Austerlitz, 13th (REASON 84)
La Palette, 43 rue de Seine, 6th (REASON 105)

Le Syndicat, 51 rue du Faubourg Saint-Denis, 10th (REASON 202)
Moonshiner, 5 rue Sedaine, 11th (REASON 225)

AFFORDABLE HOTELS
Hôtel Bedford, 17 rue de l'Arcade, 8th (REASON 154)
Hôtel Chopin, 46 Passage Jouffroy, 9th (REASON 197)
Les Piaules, 59 boulevard de Belleville, 11th (REASON 221)
Hôtel Gaston, 51 boulevard Pereire, 17th (REASON 253)
Mama Shelter, 109 rue de Bagnolet, 20th (REASON 286)

PRIVATE TERRACES
Park Hyatt, 5 rue de la Paix, 1st (REASON 1)
Sinople, 4 bis rue Saint-Sauveur, 2nd (REASON 38)
Derrière, 69 rue des Gravilliers, 3rd (REASON 50)
Grand Cœur, 41 rue du Temple, 4th (REASON 71)
Ralph's, 173 boulevard Saint-Germain, 6th (REASON 108)

BARISTA CAFÉS
Broken Arm, 12 rue Perrée, 3rd (REASON 57)
Dose, 73 rue Mouffetard, 5th (REASON 80)
Coutume, 47 rue de Babylone, 7th (REASON 134)
You Decide, 152 avenue Victor Hugo, 16th (REASON 173)
Cuillier, 19 rue Yvonne le Tac, 18th (REASON 266)

GOOD-VIBE RESTAURANTS
Ferdi, 32 rue du Mont-Thabor, 1st (REASON 9)
Cevicheria, 14 rue Bachaumont, 2nd (REASON 25)
Fish Club, 58 rue Jean-Jacques Rousseau, 1st (REASON 25)
404, 69 rue des Gravilliers, 3rd (REASON 50)
Les Bains Paris, 7 rue du Bourg-l'Abbé, 3rd (REASON 52)
Nord Marais, 39 rue Notre-Dame-de-Nazareth, 3rd (REASON 59)
La Mangerie, 7 rue de Jarente, 4th (REASON 70)
Germain, 25 rue de Buci, 6th (REASON 104)
Zo, 13 rue Montalivet, 8th (REASON 156)
Ober Mamma, 107 boulevard Richard Lenoir, 11th (REASON 213)

DETOX AND BALANCE
Fée Nature, 69 rue d'Argout, 2nd (REASON 37)
Juice It, 8 rue de la Vrillière, 1st (REASON 41)
Season, 1 rue Charles-François Dupuis, 3rd (REASON 57)
Nanashi, 57 rue Charlot, 3rd (REASON 57)
Rasa Yoga, 21 rue Saint-Jacques, 5th (REASON 86)
C'Juice, 21 rue du Dragon, 6th (REASON 94)
Marlon, 159 rue de Grenelle, 7th (REASON 133)
Thé Cool, 10 rue Jean Bologne, 16th (REASON 175)
Tigre Yoga Club, 19 rue de Chaillot, 16th (REASON 185)
Institut de Bonté, 84 quai de Jemmapes, 10th (REASON 210)

VIEWS OF PARIS
Georges, 6th floor of the Centre Pompidou, Place Georges Pompidou, 4th (REASON 72)
Hôtel Raphael, 17 avenue Kléber, 16th (REASON 170)
Les Ombres, 27 quai Branly, 7th (REASON 131)
Café de l'Homme, 17 Place du Trocadéro, 16th (REASON 181)
Déli-Cieux, 64 boulevard Haussmann, 9th (REASON 198)
Le Perchoir, 14 rue Crespin du Gast, 11th (REASON 214)
Terrass' Hôtel, 12-14 rue Joseph de Maistre, 18th (REASON 271)

BUSINESS RESTAURANTS
Water-Bar Colette, 213 rue Saint-Honoré, 1st (REASON 13)
Market, 15 avenue Matignon, 8th (REASON 161)
Laurent, 41 avenue Gabrielle, 8th (REASON 158)
Kinugawa, 1 bis rue Jean Mermoz, 8th (REASON 162)
Maison Blanche, 15 avenue Montaigne, 8th (REASON 163)
Café Kousmichoff, 71 avenue des Champs-Élysées, 8th (REASON 169)

CHARMING STREETS
Rue Mouffetard, 5th (REASON 80)
Rue Cler, 7th (REASON 135)
Rue des Marthyrs, 9th (REASON 193)
Rue Sainte-Marthe, 10th (REASON 211)
Rue de Lévis, 17th (REASON 245)

The
HEART
OF PARIS

Admire the exquisite jewelry in Place Vendôme,
take a stroll through Jardin des Tuileries and the
Louvre courtyard, visit the Musée de l'Orangerie,
savor the udon in Little Japan, enjoy an aperitif
in Little Egypt, and get a bite to eat on
the pedestrian-only streets of Montorgueil.

The Heart of Paris

17ᵉ 18ᵉ 19ᵉ
9ᵉ 10ᵉ
8ᵉ 2ᵉ 20ᵉ
16ᵉ 1ᵉʳ 3ᵉ 11ᵉ
7ᵉ 4ᵉ
6ᵉ 5ᵉ 12ᵉ
15ᵉ 14ᵉ 13ᵉ

boul. des Capucines
boul. de la Madeleine
rue des Capucines
rue Daunou
rue Volney
av. de l'Opéra
rue du 4 Septembre
rue de Choiseul
rue de la Paix
rue Gaillon
rue Monsigny
rue Sair
rue •6
rue Saint-Florentin
rue Duphot
rue Cambon
rue des-Petits-Champs
•3
4 •2
3• pl. Maurice Barrès
cour Vendôme
pl. Vendôme
•1
rue du Marché Saint-Honoré
•5
av. de l'Opéra
rue Thérèse
rue Villedo
rue de Mondovi
rue du Mont-Thabor
9
7•
rue Sainte-Anne
44• 47•
45•
46• 40•
rue Rouget de l'Isle
8•
rue de Castiglione
rue Saint-Honoré
rue Saint-Roch
4•
rue Molière
42
rue de Rivoli
rue d'Alger
10 14
rue du 29 Juillet
13•
26
rue des Pyramides
rue de Richelieu
rue de Montp
11 Jardin des Tuileries
pl. des Pyramides
16
rue de l'Échelle
pl. André Malraux
17
pl. des Colette
quai des Tuileries
rue de Rivoli
12
pl. du Palais Royal
av. du Général Lemonnier
Jardin du Carrousel
Palais du Louvre
20
pl. du Carrousel
La Pyramide
Pont Royal
quai du Louvre
Pont du Carrousel

Rubies and Vendôme

1 **Colonne Vendôme** takes center stage in this legendary square of luxury, big names in jewelry, diamonds, the Ritz and rubies. An octagonal jewel that is dreamy all day long, where Frédéric Boucheron was the first contemporary jeweler to set up shop in 1893. Walk into the heart of the **Boucheron** boutique [26 Place Vendôme, 1st], go upstairs and just watch the light. There's talk that the creator chose this specific location because the stones shine brightest at that angle. Mansion hotels surround the square. Among the most luxurious ones, **Hôtel d'Évreux** [No. 19] is a destination for Parisian high society events. In an amazing mansion hotel that was home to the Marquis de Ségur, **Van Cleef & Arpels** [No. 22] offer beginner jewelry and watchmaking classes that are open to the public (enter at 31 rue Danielle Casanova, 1st). At No. 16, you'll find the offices of well-known Japanese fashion and perfume brand, **Comme des Garçons**. For a cozy atmosphere, I recommend lunch or breakfast on **Hôtel de Vendôme**'s first floor [No. 1], comfortably seated in a great hound's-tooth armchair. A bit farther, toward the Opéra, rue de la Paix is home to **Restaurant du Park Hyatt** [5 rue de la Paix, 1st] with its sublime private terrace. A great place for a business meeting.

Kilian Hennessy
Heir to rue Cambon

2 Stylish and sleek. The black lacquer of the perfume bottles is in stark contrast to the white walls. Black and white—when it comes down to it, that's what Kilian is all about. Heir to a long line of industrialists renowned for their cognac, and grandson of the founder of the LVMH group, Kilian Hennessy managed to make a name for himself among perfume giants with his eponymous label, *by Kilian*, launched in 2006. Having mastered the artful etiquette of the highly coded Parisian upper middle class, he seduces with his piercing black eyes, his instinct for the ultimate in refinement and uncompromising openness to all that the world has to offer. When he's not in Paris with his children, or in New York with his wife, Elizabeth Jones-Hennessy, Kilian divides his time between London and Moscow, strategic centers for his fragrance business.

His creations include Good Girl Gone Bad, Liaisons Dangereuses, Cruel Intentions, Intoxicated, Light My Fire, and Smoke for the Soul. "I like to create unique combinations. The more women cultivate their sense of smell, the more familiar they will become with the variety of scents surrounding them, and they will be able to read different perfumes and how to pair them with their clothing." What do today's women look for in a perfume? Surprise? Innovation? Emotion? "Probably a bit of each," he replies, "I think women are very assertive about their autonomy, but at the same time are seeking a new romanticism and sensuality—two completely opposite values."

To discover his unique world, pay a visit to his first Parisian store, **Kilian**, on the legendary rue Cambon, the same street as **Coco Chanel's apartment**

[31 rue Cambon, 1ˢᵗ]. In this small space (only 55 square meters/592 square feet), Kilian has carefully thought through every detail, leaving nothing to chance. At the back of the store is a sofa and chair, an intimate setting where his chic clientele are invited to discover exclusive display cases and scented jewelry collections. "I always had the fantasy—the dream—of making perfume visible...thus making the invisible visible! My jewelry is a new way to wear perfume. More intimate, more precious, and without the aggressiveness of alcohol," explained the creator.

Why open a store on rue Cambon? "Of course this street is indelibly associated with Chanel—one of the finest brands in the world. There is also, importantly, the fact that it is close to the legendary rue Saint-Honoré, benefiting from its energy, while offering a little more peace and quiet." Who knows? With a bit of luck, you may even bump into Kilian. [20 rue Cambon, 1ˢᵗ]

4A 4B

The Burgundy Hotel

3 Located right by rue Saint-Honoré and rue Royale, **Le Burgundy** [6-8 rue Duphot, 1st] is charming with its absolutely wonderful restaurant beneath a glass roof. **Le Baudelaire** is a chic tearoom, champagne bar and bistronomy destination all in one. However, most appealing is its amazing pool and indoor private wellness space. A very romantic, luxurious Zen oasis in the very heart of Paris.

Domes and Bell Towers

4 Among the churches you can visit, **Notre-Dame-de-l'Assomption** (A) [263 rue Saint-Honoré, 1st] at the corner of rue Saint-Honoré and rue Cambon [Place Maurice Barrès, 1st] is one of my favorites. The funeral of famed French author Stendhal took place beneath the rotunda's sublime dome in 1842. I also like **Église Saint-Eustache** for its gothic-inspired Renaissance architecture [2 rue du Jour, 1st], **Église Saint-Roch** (B) [296 rue Saint-Honoré, 1st] for its gorgeous front square, historic paintings and tombs of famous artists, including Corneille— and **Basilique Notre-Dame-des-Victoires** [Place des Petits-Pères, 2nd] for its baroque style.

3

Place du Marché Saint-Honoré

5 From rue Saint-Honoré, turn onto rue du Marché Saint-Honoré, which leads to one of the loveliest squares in central Paris, **Place du Marché Saint-Honoré** [1st Arrondissement]. Eat on a terrace far from the urban hustle and bustle for a quiet moment in the middle of the city. Some good ideas: brunch at **Pain Quotidien** [No. 18], lunch at **Nomad's** [Nos. 12-14], happy hour at **Très Honoré** [No. 35] or dinner at **Fuxia** [No. 42], a great affordable little Italian eatery with many locations in Paris.

The square is also home to a small producers' market in a rural atmosphere in the middle of the capital. You can run your errands there on Wednesday from 12:30 p.m. to 8:30 p.m. and on Saturday from 7:00 a.m. to 3:00 p.m. You'll also find a few designer fashion shops like **Marc Jacobs** [No. 19] and **Comme des Garçons Parfums** [No. 23]. Rue du Marché Saint-Honoré has a few fun fashion accessory shops. Nearby, on rue du 29 Juillet, you'll find the delicious restaurant **Uma** [No. 7] with its Nikkei-inspired food: a mix of Peruvian and Japanese cuisines.

The square is home to a small producers' market in a rural atmosphere in the middle of the capital.

Éléphant Paname

6 A true treasure! Located between Place Vendôme and Place de l'Opéra in an old Napoleon III-style mansion hotel, **Éléphant Paname** [10 rue Volney, 2nd] is a gem for lovers of unusual cultural spots. I discovered this place during a yoga class given beneath their amazing illuminated central dome. The ceiling looks like a meteor shower with cosmic dimensions. They host dance and yoga classes, and also have a theater, an exhibition space and a fine-dining restaurant. If you're in the mood for exercising in a unique space, check out the class list posted on their website. There's also a small souvenir shop at the entrance. While you're there, try out **Bistro Volnay** on the same street [8 rue Volney, 2nd]. This excellent eatery is both modern and welcoming, serving market cuisine complemented by a wonderful wine list.

Hôtel Costes

7 Here is a legendary five-star hotel for very fashionable Parisian partyers. Established in 1995 by Jean-Louis and Gilbert Costes, **Hôtel Costes** [239-241 rue Saint-Honoré, 1st] is one of the most beautiful places to eat in the Place Vendôme area. I'm an undying fan of this one, of its muted atmosphere and rich Napoleon III decor that can only be by Jacques Garcia. Inside, a warm, slightly woody aroma seduces the senses with lounge music setting the tone. Order *"Tigre qui pleure,"* a Thai classic. You might even catch a glimpse of French celebrities, including Catherine Deneuve, Patrick Bruel or David Hallyday... Good to know: The hotel has a private pool in the basement and an absolutely incredible hammam.

Ferdi

9 It's impossible to go without at least mentioning **Ferdi** [32 rue du Mont-Thabor, 1st], a small restaurant full of charm, located right by rue Saint-Honoré. An intimate, playful and chic decor made up of small children's toys, stuffed toys (called *peluches*) and a few quotes displaying a caustic sense of humor. Who's Ferdi? He's Ferdinand, son of the owners Jacques and Alicia. Tapas vibe: Order the ceviche, tortillas, guacamole or must-try burger (voted one of the best in Paris). Alfred de Musset, the great French Romantic author ("Life is a long sleep, love is a dream and you have lived if you have loved.") died not far from here, at 6 rue du Mont-Thabor, 1st.

Underground Spas

8 Looking for a day of relaxation? The **Six Senses** spa [3 rue de Castiglione, 1st] is a Zen sanctuary located right by the Place Vendôme and Jardin des Tuileries. Inside, there's a two-story tropical wall by Patrick Blanc, oak wood cocoon stalls and the Paris sky projected in real-time in a relaxation space. Under **Hôtel Saint James Albany**'s arches [202 rue de Rivoli, 1st], you'll find the **After the Rain** spa with a 25-meter (82-foot) pool and hammam with a ceiling lit by small lights resembling a starry sky. The best plan: Book a massage and enjoy all the installations. Simply magical.

Tea at Le Meurice

10 After your stroll through Jardin des Tuileries, head to **Le Meurice** [228 rue de Rivoli, 1st]—the most beautiful palace hotel in town. Enjoy one of the best tea times in Paris—starting at 3:30 p.m.—at **Restaurant Le Dalí**, one of the hotel's two restaurants, named after the Catalan painter. They've just renovated everything! Let yourself be amazed by Alain Ducasse's majestic decor at **Restaurant Le Meurice,** the hotel's other eatery. It's a fairy tale that features antique mirrors, crystal chandeliers, marble and frescoes. Inspired by the Palace of Versailles' Salon de la Paix, Le Meurice is a museum in its own right—all the splendor that a city like Paris has to offer.

An Afternoon at the Tuileries

11

The most beautiful garden in the world is the **Tuileries** [113 rue de Rivoli, 1st], and it's the capital's oldest and greatest. As for the little story that goes along with it, the name comes from the tile manufacturers who were there in the 16th century, at the time of Catherine de Medici. From June to August, an area adjacent to rue de Rivoli is transformed into an amusement park with big rides and cotton candy. Wander around leisurely, plan a picnic or buy a sandwich at **Paul**'s near the Carrousel's archway, before grabbing a seat by a basin and taking it all in as you gaze upon Rivoli's gorgeous facades. It's an excellent spot to catch a panoramic view of Paris. I love strolling down the less crowded alleyway along the Seine and taking a bridge, any bridge, to cross to the Left Bank. You should stop off at the **Musée de l'Orangerie** to see Claude Monet's *Water Lilies* series, which was permanently installed there after the artist's death in 1927.

The Jewelry Gallery

12 For lovers of fine jewelry from the Middle Ages to now, there's a dreamy museum exhibit right by the Louvre, at the very top of the staircase in the wonderful **Musée des Arts Décoratifs** [107 rue de Rivoli, 1ˢᵗ]. The name says it all: the Galerie des Bijoux (Jewelry Gallery). About 1,200 pieces are exhibited chronologically. The first room is dedicated to the Middle Ages, followed by an amazing glass walkway that leads you to the second room, which is devoted to contemporary collections. You can also gaze upon vintage creations by Place Vendôme jewelers, including Boucheron, Cartier, Van Cleef & Arpels, Jar, Chanel and Lorenz Bäumer.

The Water-Bar Colette

13 Private, and located in the basement of **Colette** [213 rue Saint-Honoré, 1ˢᵗ]– the famous concept-store that spots trends and emerging brands worldwide– the **Water-Bar**, patronized by locals and hip travelers, is a truly pleasant spot for lunch. The menu features an endless selection of sparkling and non-sparkling water imputed with innumerable virtues, from all over the world. Beware, though! You won't be consuming only water here. The menu is rich, trendy and inventive. Each dish is a find, each dessert is from the best pastry shops in Paris (such as Paris-Brest de la Pâtisserie des Rêves, where you mustn't forget to try Jean-Paul Hévin's Mazaltov cheesecake).

"I only go to the Right Bank for Chanel, Colette and Galignani."

Karl Lagerfeld

Galignani Bookshop

14 In business for 160 years under the rue Rivoli arches, halfway between the Louvre and the Place de la Concorde, **Galignani bookshop** [224 rue de Rivoli, 1st] was devoted to English-language texts for years before opening its doors to French literature. Ernest Hemingway, Colette and Orson Welles were customers. Nowadays, you might run into Mick Jagger or Karl Lagerfeld, the latter being the most regular client of all.

Le Fumoir

15 Take a seat on the terrace or in the indoor bar for a drink at this legendary spot with a view of the Louvre. The restaurant with large windows is bright and spacious. The clientele is eclectic: very business-centric during the day and touristy at night. The food is delicious. I especially like the bookshelf at the very back. You can borrow a book to read on the spot, sitting with a cup of tea or hot chocolate with extra whipped cream [6 rue de l'Amiral Coligny, 1st].

Astier de Villatte

16 The most elegant and famous made-in-Paris ceramics in the City of Light. What will you find there? Cutlery, plates, vintage jewelry collections, candles and colognes, all made in the 13th-arrondissement workshops on boulevard Masséna. Their signature? All-white, classic and chic. You can buy scented candles with evocative names: Honolulu, Alcatraz, Alger, Delphi... And why not "rue Saint-Honoré"? [173 rue Saint-Honoré, 1st]

Place Colette

17 Look at the **Comédie-Française** facade through Murano de Jean-Michel Othoniel's fantastical aluminum and glass structure. This subway entrance at the Palais-Royal–Musée du Louvre station, called *Le Kiosque des Noctambules*, is one of my favorites in Paris. It brings a bit of color and quirkiness to the very monochrome Haussmannian style. You're at **Place Colette**, with its musicians. Tourists right in the middle of the Opéra-Louvre circuit stare at you through bus windows. Odds are you'll end up in one of their photos or they in yours. Regardless, smile! The entrance to Jardin du Palais-Royal is just steps away [Place Colette, 1st].

18 A

17   18 A

18A

A Stroll Through the Palais-Royal Garden

18 Right by the Musée du Louvre, you'll find one of Paris' most beautiful gardens, **Jardin du Palais-Royal** (A) [Place du Palais-Royal, 1st]. It has four galleries beneath archways: de Montpensier, de Beaujolais, de Valois and du Jardin. It's also a good opportunity to see the 260 shortened *Colonnes de Buren* (a piece also called *Les Deux Plateaux*), with black marble and white granite stripes. Take a reading break by the central basin that sprays its jets in a fan shape, followed by lunch on the superb Bistrot Valois terrace in a paved courtyard right next to the Passage Vérité [1 Place de Valois, 1st]. Design lovers should check out the end of this passageway with the stainless steel mesh—by architect Francis Soler—that covers the exterior of the Ministry of Culture. **Le Pain Quotidien** (B) [5 rue des Petits Champs, 1st], a restaurant located above the Galerie de Beaujolais in a historic building outside the garden, is one of my favorite places to drink an excellent latte and taste organic products, bread and all-you-can-eat chocolate toasts (*tartines*).

18B

The Louvre

19 Here is Paris' crown jewel! One of the largest museums in the world, dare I say, a castle! Take it in from the outside (it's free), walk through the Cour Napoléon, go into the Cour Carrée, the square paved courtyard right to the very back and walk all the way around. Each column, facade, statue, engraving, step or arch reveals the marvellous details of this palace with origins that go back to the 12th century. Inside, explore Western art from the Middle Ages, ancient civilizations, vestiges of moats and the dungeon of the old fortress. You could spend weeks visiting the Louvre and you wouldn't be able to see all its treasures. Some rooms aren't even open to the public. To soak in its energy, take a seat on the **Café Marly** terrace [93 rue de Rivoli, 1st] beneath the arches, which has a view of the Pyramid. Enough to make the Mona Lisa smile! [Musée du Louvre, 1st]

Carrousel du Louvre

20

Located beneath Jardin des Tuileries, the **Carrousel du Louvre** [99 rue de Rivoli, 1ˢᵗ] is a large underground shopping center to put on your list of activities for a rainy day. The **Apple Store** located beneath the Louvre's Inverted Pyramid, as well as the **Mariage Frères** tearoom, are musts. Take the stairs that lead directly into the Louvre's courtyard. Ta-dah!

Galerie Véro-Dodat's Checkerboard Floor

21 This is one of the most beautiful covered passageways in Paris. The 80-meter (262-foot) gallery, built in 1826, gets its name from its two investors, pork butcher Benoît Véro and financier Dodat. I love the black-and-white checkerboard tiling and very Parisian style. The gallery's facade on rue du Bouloi is adorned with two statues depicting Hermès and a resting satyr. This is generally the path I take: Enter at rue du Bouloi and visit the **By Terry** boutique [36 Galerie Véro-Dodat, 1st] owned by cosmetics guru Terry de Gunzburg. At the very end of the gallery, at the rue Jean-Jacques Rousseau exit, you'll find **Christian Louboutin**'s workshop/boutique [19 rue Jean-Jacques Rousseau, 1st]. You can then cross the street to **Claus** [No. 14], which is an excellent spot for a healthy breakfast or a quintessentially Parisian croissant that you can eat upstairs, away from prying eyes [Galerie Véro-Dodat, 1st].

De l'Arbre-Sec Bistros

22 Welcome to the **Garde-Robe** (A) [41 rue de l'Arbre-Sec, 1st], a rustic bistro-style cellar and food shop that strives to be the perfect spot for happy hour with friends. It's no-fuss, but they have a wide selection of natural, organic and biodynamic wines. Enjoy the Croque du Garde, a delicious Comté cheese melted onto thick and soft country-style bread that was soaked in white wine before being grilled. The concoction is then topped with a thin layer of fresh cucumber and Bayonne ham. Sinful! After your get-together, have a little walk and get to know the neighborhood. Rue de l'Arbre-Sec has an excellent selection of *terroir* cooking, like at **Racines 2** [No. 39], David Lanher's second establishment after his restaurant Racines in the Passage des Panoramas. You'll recognize the legendary Starck-designed deer antlers. The open, personal-chef-style stainless steel kitchen has a long communal table in the middle of the room. Fish, fresh herbs and crunchy veggies adorn your plate, while natural wines fill up your glass, all for €40 per person. Good to know: **L'Empire** hotel [No. 48], along with being centrally located, is pretty good in the boutique hotel category, and it has its own sauna-hammam.

21 22A

Sunset at Square du Vert-Galant

23 If you're in the 1st Arrondissement near Châtelet, cross the **Pont Neuf**: a monument in its own right. It's the oldest bridge in Paris, the longest in the heart of the city (238 m/781 ft) and the first with sidewalks to protect pedestrians from mud and horses. Go curl up in one of its alcoves and get lost in the beautiful view of the Seine. Then, stop at **Place Dauphine** on Île de la Cité, a lovely triangular space where one of the points leads to the middle of Pont Neuf. It's one of Paris' five royal squares. You'll find art galleries and a few small restaurant-cafés away from the hustle and bustle of crowds. U2 singer Bono's old apartment stands at 14 on Place Dauphine, 1st. Now, it's a prestigious venue reserved for private events. The panoramic view offers a glimpse of Place Dauphine and the Eiffel Tower on one side and the Seine and Louvre on the other. Finish off your stroll at the **Square du Vert-Galant** at the island's western point. Buy some sushi, a bottle of rosé and take advantage of the city on the cheap as you watch the shuttle boats. An irresistible cliché.

Village Montorgueil

24 Rue Montorgueil is one of my favorite streets in Paris. Pass under the archway of rue des Petits Carreaux (an extension of Montorgueil), breathe in the smell of flowers, bread, croissants, fresh fruit, fish... I love the atmosphere of this pedestrian walkway that plunges you into historic Paris. Try out **Little Italy** (A) [92 rue Montorgueil, 2nd], a pleasant Italian eatery. **Stohrer** (B) [No. 51], established in 1730, is the oldest pastry shop in Paris; their specialty is the *puits d'amour*—a pastry filled with redcurrant jelly or raspberry jam. The **Au Rocher de Cancale** restaurant [No. 78] is registered as a historic monument; you can still see frescoes by Paul Giovanni (1804-1866) there. Au Rocher de Cancale's old location (across the street) was a go-to for Balzac and Alexandre Dumas. **Compas** [No. 62], with its sunny terrace, is a fave. They serve tasty Parisian classics in a historical environment that's charming. The **Passage du Grand-Cerf** [145 rue Saint-Denis, 2nd] houses the works of all sorts of creators, artisans, decorators and fashion designers.

Nautical Bistros

25 The Montorgueil area is an excellent meeting spot for dinner with friends. Among the new restaurants, the trend is nautically inclined. First off, **La Marée Jeanne** [3 rue Mandar, 2nd] with its navy blue facade and giant fish sets the tone for this wave of nautical bistros. On the menu: fried smelt, a lobster croque, oysters (obviously) and mixed seafood platters. **Cevicheria** [14 rue Bachaumont, 2nd] specializes in raw fish marinated in *leche de tigre* (lime, garlic, hot pepper, ginger). **Fish Club** [58 rue Jean-Jacques Rousseau, 1st] is located just a few doors down.

Chantal Thomass
High priestess of "pin-up" lingerie

➤➤ ॰ ⬅⬅

26 While the lingerie certainly stands on its own, there's also the woman behind it— Chantal Thomass: high priestess of undergarments, Parisian lingerie icon. With her bone-straight black hair, angular bangs, black skirt and jacket, white shirt and bright red lips, her look is unmistakable. An erotic realm, her storefront on rue Saint-Honoré is legendary: Women (and men!) come from all around the world to admire her lingerie.

She began her design career at the end of the 1960s, at a time when women were feeling less inhibited and tended not to wear bras.

"There was no such things as women's seductive lingerie. I came after the feminists who rejected bras. I was fascinated by the lingerie from the 1930s and '40s: the cone bras, garters and extravagant negligees. That era was the inspiration for my ready-to-wear designs."

And so she launched her ready-to-wear brand Ter et Bantine. Her fans include icons, like Brigitte Bardot, who are smitten by her playful and bohemian style: ribbons, Chantilly lace, flannel bodices, and suede or satin corsets worn over men's shirts. Thomass is the one who turned lingerie into a fashion item. Her trademark—bright colors, pink lace over red backgrounds, garters peeking through a slit skirt, and bras exposed by an open shirt—is a mix of seduction and impertinence.

"There's always a touch of humor, fun and originality. But I never veer into the vulgar—that's a line I never cross," she explained. What's her inspiration? "Old lace, for example, transformed into contemporary lace designs. Corsets from the early 1900s. For an evening out, corsets are extremely flattering. And materials, too: tulle and lace for transparency. I love Chantilly lace, the one Empress Eugénie, wife of Napoleon III, adored. And Leavers lace, the most delicate and expensive."

Her favorite colors? "Black and pink. Black because it shows off the figure, and pink is very flattering and gives people a healthy glow." Thomass has special insight into what is concealed under a woman's clothing: "It's very surprising. I've seen extremely traditional women in their little suits buy really sexy and original lingerie, and I've seen bona fide fashionistas who only wear standard Calvin Klein underwear. It's a question of personality. It's not easy to find what suits you... You have to take a good look in the mirror and examine both your good features and your flaws, highlight the good and hide the less good." What's her favorite piece of lingerie? "Bras, because you can play with both shape and color. They showcase the breasts, so they are very important." Her best advice on seduction? "You need to seduce yourself first, before seducing others." **Chantal Thomass** [211 rue Saint-Honoré, 1st].

Passage des Panoramas

27 One of the few surviving pedestrian arcades in Paris, Passage des Panoramas attracts foodie-addict locals, first and foremost to **Noglu** [No. 16], the gluten-free must-try. On one side, there's the neo-bistro restaurant with its long table, while on the other, you'll find a caterer selling gluten-free breads, muffins, pastries and other treats. Their slogan? "At Noglu, *everything is gluten free!*" (Yes, it is written in English!) **Caffè Stern** [No. 47] is a gourmet Italian spot located in an old historic Parisian printer's shop that was redecorated by Philippe Starck. The woodwork is from the 17th century and the wooden floors are original. Request a table in the sublime back lounge. Farther down the passageway, you'll come across **Coinstot Vino** [Nos. 25-26], where they serve a wonderful selection of natural wines (Ardèche, Bourgogne, Alsace, Jura, etc.) and charcuterie boards to enjoy on the covered terrace; a unique find [Passage des Panoramas, 2nd].

Nose

28 We're at **Nose** [20 rue Bachaumont, 2nd], right in the heart of the Montorgueil area, on rue Bachaumont. Here, get your hands on some perfume from the refined selection of fragrances. To help your decision-making, this spot innovates with their olfactory diagnosis to determine your personal olfactory pyramid. Name? Birthday? Olfactory background? Favorite notes? The point: to draw up a list of ingredients that overlap in your favorite perfumes and create the olfactory pyramid you want with a custom-made selection, using only an iPad and your nose.

Hôtel Bachaumont

29 Those looking for a contemporary hotel with a classic Parisian twist will find **Hôtel Bachaumont** [18 rue Bachaumont, 2nd] an excellent choice. The hotel, which gets its name from the scandalous 18th-century French writer Louis Petit de Bachaumont, was a Paris institution in the Roaring Twenties. In time, it became the "Clinique Bachaumont," before the legendary spot made its comeback with great pomp in July 2015 after massive renovations. Inside the restaurant, the handmade marble mosaic floor is an exact replica of the cobblestone pattern on rue Montorgueil. At night, have a drink at the **Night Flight** bar (a homage to Saint-Exupéry's novel *Vol de Nuit*) and enjoy the copper-colored velvet seats, low totemic black wooden tables and round poufs. The hotel has 49 rooms (17-50 m²/ 183-538 ft²). I adore the fabric headboards designed by the rue du Mail institution, **Pierre Frey** [No. 27].

Stock Gerard Darel

30 One of the greatest joys for Parisian women is to find the capital's best outlets. In the Sentier neighborhood, you'll come across the **Stock Gerard Darel** [19 rue du Sentier, 2nd], a famed French brand with classic, chic and laid-back cuts. To access the shop, go into the building's yard, take the first door on the left and head upstairs. You'll find 300 square meters (3,200 ft²) of blouses, dresses, skirts, pants, jeans, leggings, trenches and coats. Sale prices can go down to 30 percent of the listed in-store price. Nothing old, only the season's collections.

Experimental Cocktail Club

31 This is one of the best cocktail bars in the neighborhood for enjoying the Parisian-style art of mixology in a snug lounge setting. Head over on a weekday for happy hour or an after-dinner drink with a small group, as this place has very few seats– on weekends when there's a DJ, you may have to get real cozy. The bartenders and their shakers are sure to give you an eyeful [37 rue Saint-Sauveur, 2nd].

*At night, have a drink at the **Night Flight** bar (a homage to Saint-Exupéry's novel* Vol de Nuit*).*

HOTEL BACHAUMONT

PASSAGE DU CAIRE

Little Egypt

32 Du Caire, du Nil, d'Aboukir and d'Alexandrie streets...
Here you are in Little Egypt, a part of Paris right in the middle of the Sentier neighborhood, known for its "hot" textiles. Behind the scenes, in the wings of pedestrian-only rue des Petits Carreaux, is where many wholesalers, accessory and ready-to-wear producers work. The shop windows could use some love—everything is crumbling and the goods are far from Parisian chic. **Passage du Caire** [Place du Caire, 2nd], inaugurated in 1798 during Napoleon's Egyptian campaign, is the oldest covered passageway in Paris. Although slightly rundown at the moment, it's a location that will most likely change in the coming years. A detour while on a stroll is worth it, mostly to witness the evolution of a dynamic neighborhood.

2e Arrt
RUE D'ALEXANDRIE

2e Arrt
PLACE DU CAIRE

Du Nil Street

33

To get your French attitude, explore rue du Nil just north of rue Réaumur. Du Nil is a 72-meter-long (236-foot) micro-street that attracts the Parisian crowd that hangs out at the famous restaurant **Frenchie** [No. 5], a "neo-institution." It's impossible to get a table and that's just fine, since it gives you a good reason to try out **Frenchie to Go** [No. 9], where they serve high-quality street food. Order a lobster roll or the beloved fish & chips. Even better: Grab a drink at **Frenchie Wine Bar** [No. 6] in a relaxed vibe surrounded by locals right across the street. To impress your guests, go shop at the **Terroirs d'Avenir** boutique [Nos. 6-8], nicknamed the "spot for multi-starred chefs, where " you might run into Paris' greatest avant-garde chefs: Alain Ducasse, David Toutain (7th), Bertrand Grébaud (Septime, 11th). What is it? A grocery, butcher shop and fish store all rolled into one, where they promote local dietary biodiversity. The owners—members of the Slow Food Movement—are supporters of sustainable culture, respect for the environment and seasonality. You'll therefore find the most delicious seasonal products, older vegetable varieties, "purebred" meat, sustainably fished seafood and organic cheese, all at reasonable prices. This narrow Sentier street has by far the best reputation when it comes to sustainable gastronomy [rue du Nil, 2nd].

Aboukir Oasis

34 One of the most beautiful green walls in Paris, also called **L'Oasis d'Aboukir** [at the corner of rue d'Aboukir and rue des Petits Carreaux, 2nd], is 25 meters high (82 ft) and is home to over 7,600 plants from 237 species. A genius display of botanical design by Patrick Blanc, "the one who reintroduces nature where we least expect it."

Edgar Hotel

35 Located steps away from rue Montorgueil on a charming square in the heart of Little Egypt, away from all the buzz, you'll find **Hôtel Edgar** [31 rue d'Alexandrie, 2nd]. This boutique hotel has a very Parisian, quirky feel. Each room is unique and was decorated by a guest artist. The terrace is also an excellent happy hour meeting spot. Cross the street and go straight to **Baretto di Edgar** restaurant [No. 14], a charming pizzeria trattoria that belongs to the owners of Edgar.

"God invented Parisians so that foreigners wouldn't understand the people of France."

Alexandre Dumas fils

Silencio at Night

36 To embrace the pleasures of the Parisian night after midnight, head straight to **Silencio** [142 rue Montmartre, 2nd], filmmaker David Lynch's club established in 2011. Hidden away in a private basement, this unusual place has a smoking room, library/bookstore, concert stage, photo gallery and projection room. It belongs to its members from 6 p.m. to 11 p.m. and then opens its door to clubbers and the Right Bank boho-style night owls.

The Nature Fairy

37 It's my favorite spot for a healthy, affordable and simple lunch. Quinoa, quiches, freshly pressed vegetable juices... At **Fée Nature** [69 rue d'Argout, 2nd], everything is absolutely delicious, organic, healthy and made on the premises. Their philosophy ("Eat well to live better") prevails in each dish made with love. Next door, **Leoni's Deli** [No. 67] serves organic hot dogs with organic meat and buns. **Fée Nature** has another location in the 10th Arrondissement [40 bis rue du Faubourg Poissonnière].

Montorgueil's Eden

38 A small green haven hidden in a courtyard, the Sinople is surprising with its Brazilian oasis airs: palm trees, cacti and vintage decor... The retractable glass roof allows diners to eat beneath the stars regardless of the weather. It's also the best place to watch the comings and goings of Paris' hottest athletes, since it's also the restaurant of the Parisian elite sports club, **Klay** [4 bis rue Saint-Sauveur, 2nd]. Try the sea-bream ceviche, crusted fresh cod (*cabillaud*) or must-try Sinople Burger.

A Burger Facing Molière

40 Not far from the Palais-Royal, at the intersection of rue Richelieu, rue Molière and rue Thérèse, is a miniscule square that's home to the **Fontaine Molière** [Place Mireille]. Erected in 1844, it is close to the place where the famous playwright died at the age of 51 in 1673, just a few hours after his last staging of *Malade Imaginaire*. Stop in at **Hand** [39 rue de Richelieu, 1st], an American restaurant that Parisians are crazy about. Have a seat at the window-facing bar to gaze upon the impressive Molière statue as you enjoy a juicy cheeseburger and onion rings. It's a fun way of combining a cultural visit with decadent delight. FYI: Molière has remained the most played and read comedy author of French literature since the 17th century.

David Mallett

39 Here's a destination that travels word-of-mouth when you're in cahoots with people in the high-end fashion world. David Mallett arrived in Paris at the age of 27 and opened the doors to his "apartment" hair salon in 2004. Now, the huge private salon in Haussmannian style has tripled in size. People love the small terrace where you can sip coffee during a dye break, the custom-made treatments and the unusual presence of a stuffed ostrich. For a cut, ask for Rishi who styles hair for the greatest shows at Paris Fashion Week or, obviously, the star hairdresser David himself [14 rue Notre-Dame-des-Victoires, 2nd].

Place des Victoires

41 Between rue Montorgueil and Place des Victoires, there's a nice selection of fashion boutiques. To complete your shopping spree, continue your stroll to the elegant, circular **Place des Victoires**—one of my favorites in Paris—where the glorious equestrian statue of Louis XIV is erected. There, you'll find fashion designers like **Kenzo** [No. 3] or **Yohji Yamamoto** [25 rue du Louvre, 1st]. **Hôtel Charlemagne** [No. 1] is a mansion hotel registered as a historical monument. On a small adjacent street, the **Juice It** counter [8 rue de la Vrillière, 1st] isn't eye-catching at first glance. But if you look closely, you'll see a few pineapple leaves and other fruits and veggies in the window... indicating freshly pressed juice for sale. Inside, there's a long counter, a few stools, juice, raw salads and other sprouts, all to go.

43 A 43 B

Café-Baguette

42 Discovering Paris also means falling for the famous café-baguette morning tradition. Nicknamed the "Canadian café" because of its rustic decor, **Baguett's Café** [33 rue de Richelieu, 1st] updates the art of French tradition of breakfasting on a fresh baguette, compulsory croissant, jams and Nutella, with coffee, hot chocolate or tea for dipping. That's how you start the day off right.

43 C

The Vivienne Spirit

43 The Palais-Royal's neighborhoods are home to the charming **Galerie Vivienne** (A) [6 rue Vivienne, 2nd], a not-to-be-missed covered passageway. In rainy weather or during the winter, the gallery is lit and heated. Grab a bite to eat amid the 19th-century decor at **Bistrot Vivienne** [4 rue des Petits Champs, 2nd]. It is open seven days a week, which is rather rare in Paris. The restaurant's first floor is classically Parisian with red velvet armchairs and antique mirrors. Inside the gallery, you'll find **Legrand Filles & Fils** [1 rue de la Banque, 2nd], a good destination to enjoy an excellent selection of wines. They also have their own shop and wine school. One block farther, you have to stop beneath the glass dome in the rotunda of **Galerie Colbert**, another gorgeous Parisian covered arcade. The brasserie **Le Grand Colbert** (B) [2 rue Vivienne, 2nd] is a legendary Paris spot that's often used to shoot films. Still on rue Vivienne, the headquarters of fashion house **Céline** (C) have been located in the beautiful 17th-century mansion hotel [No. 16], the old Hôtel Colbert de Torcy, since 2014. The workshops are located on the top floor, below the glass roof.

Little Japan

44 Is an Eastern wind blowing through the streets of Paris? No. The so-called "Japanese of rue Sainte-Anne, " better known as Little Japan, is the golden block of Parisian ramen. The traditional Japanese dish is making a splash here. In 2014, Paris actually inaugurated its first "Ramen Week," during which eight great Japanese chefs serve up their best ramen all around town. For a Tokyo vibe, go to **Sapporo** [37 rue Sainte-Anne, 1st] or to the small **Kotteri Ramen Naritake** [31 rue des Petits Champs, 1st] and take a seat at the counter. Super comforting, exotic and very affordable.

Udon Bistro

45 Younger brother of the legendary Little Japan eatery **Kunitoraya** [5 rue Villedo, 1st], **Udon Bistro Kunitoraya** [1 rue Villedo, 1st] is my local fave. Long and narrow with wooden tables, stools and brick walls, it plunges you into an airy New-York vibe where you'll want to eat a bowl of udon (traditional fat Japanese noodles made with flour, water and salt). Order a bowl of homemade udon served with cold sauce or in a hot broth, topped with fried tofu, quail eggs and seaweed. The chef's recommendation? The Kunitora udon with minced pork, radishes and salsify in a warm miso broth. Respect the house rules: "Eat the udon as you sip it or sip it as you eat." Slurp!

Japanese Bakery

46 Right in the heart of the Japanese neighborhood, **Aki Boulanger** [16 rue Sainte-Anne, 1st] serves fusion creations that mix traditional French baking and Japanese specialties. Among the must-tries: matcha green tea tiramisu, kabuki green tea opera cake, yuzu éclair, azuki Paris-Brest. And don't forget the melon brioche bread and milk green tea biscuits. Good to know: They also serve breakfast. Bentos and sandwiches can be eaten on the premises.

Neo-Café

47 Nestled in the heart of the Japanese quarter and Palais-Royal, the **Télescope** café [5 rue Villedo, 1ˢᵗ] is part of the new wave of modern Parisian coffee shops. Far from the traditional café-terrace, this space is made up of long counters and a few tables (and only 10 seats). With a pastel beige, airy and chic facade, it's a neighborhood haunt known by word of mouth for its excellent coffee (filter, espresso, hazelnut, cream) and cookies: Enjoy a break away from Paris' busy streets.

Centr'Halles Park

48 **Canopée** is the new "belly of Paris." The green oasis strives to be a place dedicated to children, culture and urban activities, while also being a commercial temple. After years of demolition, the giant hole that was once the Forum des Halles reopened in Spring 2016, entirely renovated with a chicer, hipper spirit focused on Parisian fashion. Lovers of shopping can expect 130 boutiques and a "canopy"—a steel and glass roof that covers the space. Eat at the Alain Ducasse **Restaurant Champeaux** [101 rue Berger, 1ˢᵗ], directly beneath the canopy, and stop at ZA, Fabienne and Philippe Amzalak's literary café, designed by Philippe Starck. In the garden, outside the canopy, try an activity that's unique to Paris: Parkour, the sport that was born in Paris in the 1980s. The manifesto: getting from point A to point B as efficiently and quickly as possible on an obstacle course. Running, jumping, climbing, balancing and acrobatics: a good program indeed.

48

UPPER MARAIS
and
AVANT-GARDE FASHION

Find "bobo" (bourgeois-bohemian) boutiques
in the Upper Marais (Haut-Marais), explore the new
Carreau du Temple, soak up the sights, sounds
and smells of the marketplace at the Marché
des Enfants Rouges, (re)discover the incomparable
Place des Vosges and enjoy the gentle charms
of Île Saint-Louis.

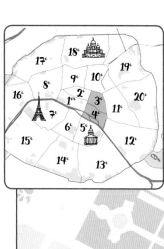

Upper Marais and Avant-Garde Fashion

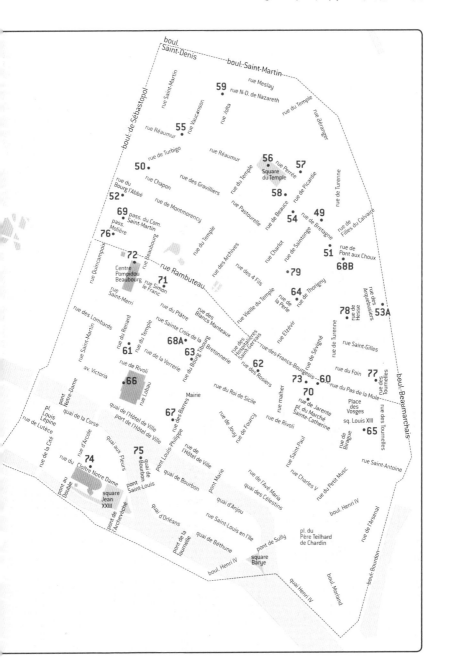

boul. Saint-Denis

boul. Saint-Martin

rue Meslay

59
rue N-D. de Nazareth

rue Saint-Martin

rue Vaucanson

rue du Temple

rue Joita

rue de l'Éranger

55
rue Réaumur

rue de Turbigo

rue Réaumur

56
rue Perrée

57

boul. de Sébastopol

50
rue Chapon

rue des Gravilliers

Square du Temple

rue du Temple

rue de Picardie

rue de Turenne

rue du Bourg l'Abbé

52

rue de Montmorency

58

rue Pastourelle

rue de Beauce

54
rue de Saintonge

49

rue de Bretagne

rue de Filles du Calvaire

69
pass. du Com. Saint-Martin

pass. Molière

76

rue Beaubourg

rue du Temple

rue des Archives

rue Charlot

51
rue de Pont aux Choux

68B

72

Centre Pompidou Beaubourg

rue Rambuteau

rue des 4 Fils

79

64
rue de Thorigny

rue de la Perle

rue des Arquebusiers

71
rue Simon le Franc

rue Saint-Merri

rue du Plâtre

rue Vieille du Temple

rue Elzévir

78
rue de Hesse

53A

rue Quincampoix

rue des Lombards

rue du Renard

rue Sainte Croix de la Bretonnerie

rue des Blancs Manteaux

rue des Hospitalières St-Gervais

rue de Sévigné

rue de Turenne

rue Saint-Gilles

rue Saint-Martin

rue du Temple

68A

63
rue du Bourg Tibourg

rue des Francs-Bourgeois

rue du Foin

77
rue des Tournelles

av. Victoria

61
rue de la Verrerie

62
rue des Rosiers

73 **60**
rue du Pas de la Mule

boul. Beaumarchais

pl. Louis Lépine

rue de Lutéce

pont Notre-Dame

quai de la Corse

66
rue Lobau

Mairie

rue du Roi de Sicile

rue malher

70
rue de Jarente

pl. du Marché Sainte-Catherine

Place des Vosges

sq. Louis XIII

rue des Tournelles

rue de la Cité

rue du

pont d'Arcole

67
rue des Barres

rue Jouy

rue de Fourcy

rue de Rivoli

rue Saint-Paul

rue de Birague

65

quai aux Fleurs

75
quai de Bourbon

pont Louis-Philippe

rue de Jouy

rue de l'Hôtel de Ville

quai de Bourbon

pont Marie

rue de l'Ave Maria

rue Charles V

rue du Petit Musc

rue Saint-Antoine

port de l'Hôtel de Ville

74
Cloître Notre Dame

pont Saint-Louis

pont au Double

square Jean XXIII

rue de l'Hôtel de Ville

pont de l'Archevêché

quai d'Orléans

quai d'Anjou

quai des Célestins

boul. Henri IV

rue Saint-Paul

pont de la Tournelle

quai de Saint-Louis en l'Ile

quai de Béthune

pont de Sully

pl. du Père Teilhard de Chardin

rue de l'Arsenal

boul. Henri IV

square Barye

boul. Morland

boul. Bourdon

quai Henri IV

Clandestine SOMA

49

Located south of the Marais (SOMA for South Marais), **Candelaria** [52 rue de Saintonge, 3rd] is one of the most unusual cocktail bars in all of Paris. But first, you'll have to find it! Spot the "tacos" sign, a little hole-in-the-wall taqueria (taco restaurant) with a southern, Mexican vibe. You might think you're in the wrong place, and that's exactly the point! Walk through the door at the very back: That's where you'll find the cocktail bar. The concept was inspired by clandestine bars where secret parties took place during the Prohibition. A cozy vibe starts off the night, turning more festive around 10 p.m. The **Ob-La-Di coffee shop** [No. 54] right next door is also worth the trip for their homemade jams and avocado toast—and its black-and-white tiles. On the same street, **SÔMA** [No. 13] is a Japanese neo-bistro that made quite a splash—thanks to Laos-born chef, Sourasack Phongphet, a neighborhood star. Shrimp tempura, mackerel tartare with shiso leaves, sashimi, seaweed salad, sake-steamed shells and Franco-Japanese French toast for dessert. Take a seat at the counter to catch every second of the culinary show!

The Gems of Rue des Gravilliers

50 This small street isn't much to look at, but it still has three unique spots that are worth the trip. My favorite Moroccan restaurant is **404** [No. 69]. They serve the best lamb tagine, lemon chicken and Berber couscous in a North African ambiance with incredible stone decor. It's a trip in and of itself, and I highly recommend making a reservation. You can book the small lounge on the 2nd floor (10 seats) for a birthday with guaranteed atmosphere. Located in 404's backyard, **Derrière** certainly doesn't lack originality. You can eat in different rooms of the house (living room, bedroom, kitchen). There's an old wooden cabinet on the 2nd floor: Open the door, cross over and step into a smoking room with the baroque style of an old castle. **La Trinquette** [No. 67] is a wine shop that specializes in Languedoc wines. Go for a happy hour drink and a French cheese and charcuterie board. This spot is located in an old, historic factory that made canes and umbrella handles [Rue des Gravilliers, 3rd].

The Destination Shop

51 The multi-brand trend—so-called concept stores, where it's fun to wander and discover gems—is gaining more and more converts in Paris. Among the names to remember: **FrenchTrotters** [128 rue Vieille du Temple, 3rd], a concept launched by Carole and Clarent Dehlouz in 2005. Located in the heart of Upper Marais, their second two-story boutique has a nice selection of men and women's clothing, design objects, cosmetics, magazines and shoes. The boutique also has its own ready-to-wear brand, including a denim line, all of which is made in Paris.

A Nighttime Dip

52 The legendary old Parisian nightclub, Les Bains Paris (called Les Bains) shut down in 2010 before making a big comeback with a highly stylized and complete redesign. This place is a restaurant, spa and hotel all in one. Start with a meal at **La Salle-à-Manger** [7 rue du Bourg-l'Abbé, 3rd] with its glossy, burgundy decor. For mains, try the exquisite pak choi monkfish medallion with a kefir tea before heading to the basement to dance on the chic black-and-white checkerboard floor designed by Philippe Starck. The blue hammam-pool (the spot's original) is still in the club. A few glasses of champagne and...splash! Waterproof makeup is indispensible.

Conceptual Nutrition

53 In the heart of the Marais, new grocery stores are revisiting the supermarket concept. That's the case at **Bien l'Épicerie** [20 rue Saint-Gilles, 3rd], a gourmet food store that specializes in organic and natural products. **Maison Plisson** (A) [93 boulevard Beaumarchais, 3rd] is also worth mentioning. They have charcuterie, a wine cellar, cheese shop, café, terrace and takeout counter. Fare is chosen by blind tastings with the best farmers and producers in France and Europe. Most of the products are exclusive to Paris. Be sure to stop in at the famous **Merci** [No. 111] concept shop, the solidarity store where 100 percent of the profits are donated to organizations—via a foundation—that help women and children in Madagascar. Get your hands on a few fashion and design exclusives and browse the three floors brightened by a massive skylight. Their café stocks 10,000 used books. A few steps away, you'll find **Grazie** [No. 91], one of my favorite Paris pizzerias due to its industrial decor and New-York spirit.

53 A

Enfants Rouges Souk

54 Looking for your senses to take you on a trip to a multicultural souk right in the middle of bobo Haut Marais? Established in 1628, **Marché des Enfants Rouges** [39 rue de Bretagne, 3ʳᵈ] is Paris' oldest covered market. I love having lunch on the terrace or going for weekend brunch with friends. I recommend the Moroccan caterer's tagines and couscous, Taeko's Japanese bentos and pasta at Mangiamo Italiano. Take a seat at a table, soak in the moment and forget everything else. The vibe is laid-back and unique. While you're there, run some errands or buy flowers or spices. There are also good foodie destinations in the area like **Mmmozza** [57 rue de Bretagne, 3ʳᵈ], a small cheese shop that specializes in Italian mozzarella and di bufala burrata that you can enjoy on the premises or take to go. To die for.

56

The Arty Metro

55 While some metro stations are awful, smelly and decrepit, others put us at peace with public transit. Among my faves in the Paris Metro? The Arts et Métiers station in the 3rd Arrondissement is made of streamlined copper, has a sci-fi feel and was designed by artist François Schuiten. It feels like being in a submarine with portholes. From there, you can visit the **Musée des Arts et Métiers** [60 rue Réaumur, 3rd], located in the Saint-Martin-des-Champs abbey. It specializes in the history of the city's industrial techniques and heritage.

Upper Marais' Lungs

56 In this central part of Paris where there is very little green space, **Square du Temple** [64 rue de Bretagne, 3rd] is therefore like a fresh oasis of oxygen. Take a break on a park bench or the lawn by a fountain or pool. Notice the sumptuous architecture of the Haussmannian buildings through the foliage. The trees are beautiful and notably include Turkish hazel, ginkgo biloba and Chinese cedar. The square was named an "ecological green space" by Écocert in 2007.

55

The Bobo Square

57 Behind the hustle and bustle of rue de Bretagne, you'll find a square that I really like, the **Carreau du Temple**, not least because of the amazing glass-covered metal structure from the 19th century that has been newly restored–a high-end location for fashion events, shows and exhibits of all kinds. Small restaurants and trendy concept boutiques have set up shop all around. **Mme Shawn** [18 rue Caffarelli, 3rd] is a delicious, iconic Thai restaurant, and **PNY** (**Paris New York**) (A) [1 rue Perrée, 3rd] is the hamburger specialist's third location in Paris. The pink flamingo decor is reminiscent of retro Hollywood diners. Try the house classic: The Return of the Cowboy. The very bright and design-focused **Broken Arm** (B) [12 rue Perrée, 3rd] is a concept store filled with handpicked clothing, books, furniture and shoes where you can also get a little something to eat. **Le Barav** [6 rue Charles-François Dupuis, 3rd] is worth it for their good wines and charcuterie boards. **Season** [1 rue Charles-François Dupuis], with its airy Scandinavian style, is a hybrid between a juice bar, neo-bistro and takeout counter. The menu was created by an English chef and naturopath who specializes in gluten-free fare. **Nanashi** [57 rue Charlot, 3rd] is at the top of the list for Japanese bento in an airy Parisian setting. Try the institution **Café Pinson** [6 rue du Forez, 3rd] for a salad or healthy juice in a hip, laid-back atmosphere. **Les Chouettes** [32 rue de Picardie, 3rd], previously Café Rouge, has also had a makeover in the last few years. They now attract the golden youth with their two-story, 20-meter high (66-foot) Eiffel backdrop and gorgeous glass roof.

Rue de Bretagne

58 Rue de Bretagne is the Haut Marais' epicenter: a classic Parisian commercial street with a cheese monger, butcher, bookstore, cafés, terraces... There's a young bobo atmosphere and you'll cross paths with people in the fashion, design and film world. **Chez Omar** [No. 47] is a legendary local spot known for serving some of the best couscous in the city in a Parisian brasserie setting. **Bontemps** pastry shop (A) [No. 57] specializes in many variations of stuffed shortbread, while **Café Charlot** [No. 38] acts as the headquarters for the area's locals. Its sunny terrace is the ideal spot to see and be seen, to capture the neighborhood's vibrant energy and remake the world at all hours of the day. Secondhand sales in the spring and fall attract crowds of bargain hunters and shrewd collectors. At the very end of the street, at the corner of rue Vielle du Temple, you'll find bistro **Le Progrès'** terrace [No. 1], a high-end gathering spot for Marais' youth to enjoy a boozy happy hour in a great atmosphere, with mixed food boards on the side: Pierre Warren, the chef, developed his skill with star chef Hélène Darroze [Rue de Bretagne, 3rd].

NOMA's Creators

59 To get your hands on the brands of small-scale designers, I recommend going up into NOMA (Nord du Marais) to discover rue Notre-Dame-de-Nazareth, an old textile commercial street located right by Place de la République. This emerging street overflows with creative and alternative projects. **Beau Bien** [No. 21], a multi-brand boutique, has a good selection of hot menswear. At **Wait** [No. 9], you'll walk into a shop with a surfer vibe, creative wooden eyeglasses and lines made exclusively in Brittany. The **LO/A** [No. 17] bookshop is filled with old and contemporary works to feed the creativity of trend-seekers. **Nord Marais** (A) [No. 39] is a must-try restaurant and go-to canteen for the local artsy fashion crowd. In the evening, you can try excellent tapas and mixed boards.

58A 59A

Nord Marais

60 61A

Bourgeois Shopping

60

Le Marais is undergoing huge changes and is increasingly being taken over by luxury brands. It's actually called the "New Golden Triangle," and is therefore not the place to hunt for deals, but rather to window-shop in a maze of streets that feel like a museum. While rue des Archives is home to fashion brands like **Givenchy** [No. 13] and **Fendi** [No. 9], rue des Francs Bourgeois is the new destination for high-end beauty. **Chanel** laid claim to it with its beauty-boutique, alongside **Guerlain, Diptyque, Jo Malone, L'Occitane, Kiehl's, Mac** and **Bobbi Brown** [between Nos. 1 and 17, rue des Francs Bourgeois, 4th]. Less flashy and more natural, **Huygens** (A) [24 rue du Temple, 4th] is a Parisian brand to discover. In a laboratory setting, they sell skin-care products mixed with the essential oils of your choosing.

Best Vintage Shops

61

There are plenty of vintage shops in the Marais, providing bargain hunters with some great finds. The most famous among them is **Free'P'Star** [20 rue de Rivoli, 4th]: a true jumble of bags, boots and vintage dresses straight out of old closets! The shop smells like old trunk bottoms. Prices are affordable and, if your timing is right, you can find nice pieces. The concept at **Kilo Shop** (A) [69-71 rue de la Verrerie, 4th] is the only one of its kind: Rather than pricing each individual item, you pay for your clothes by weight (€30 per kilo of dresses and €20 per kilo of T-shirts). It could take up a few hours of your time...if you like to rummage!

Like in Tel Aviv

62 Located in the heart of Pletzl, Paris' Jewish quarter, **Miznon** [22 rue des Écouffes, 4th] is said to be the best new pita place in Paris. Miznon? It means "buffet" in Hebrew. The menu is written on a big board, you order and once your pita (or *pitot*) is ready, they call your name. My heart is torn between the lamb kebab and the chocolate-banana pita! This area is also right in the heart of the golden falafel block. **L'As du Fallafel** [32-34 rue des Rosiers, 4th] is a legendary local eatery that can be found in guidebooks worldwide, along with many other "falafel kings" who share the booty of the abundance of lovers of pitot with chickpea balls. Eat it on the spot amid the bustling crowd or on a quiet bench in the rose garden **Jardin des Rosiers** [10 rue des Rosiers, 4th].

Bourg Tibourg Hotel

63 For people who love boutique hotels and the cozy, opulent style of architect and decorator Jacques Garcia, **Bourg Tibourg** Hotel [19 rue du Bourg Tibourg, 4th] is an intimate little 30-room cocoon that's rather small, but very charming. A real gem with refined, elegant and warm details that will make you want to savor a cognac or glass of champagne while reading a book from the shelf: Marcel Proust, Oscar Wilde, Jean Cocteau.

65

Picasso Museum

64 While the Marais wasn't a museum destination before, **Musée Picasso** has literally changed the game since opening in 2014. Located in Hôtel Salé [5 rue de Thorigny, 3rd], one of the grandest 17th-century mansion hotels, it recounts the history and influence of the sculptor, ceramist, painter, writer and photography genius chronologically from one floor to the next. The historical location, which has been entirely reworked, has over 5,000 pieces—ranging from some of the artist's major works to other lesser-known pieces—exhibited in 37 rooms. The vaulted cellars are particularly impressive.

Victor Hugo's Spirit

65 In the heart of the gorgeous Place des Voges is where writer Victor Hugo wrote many of his works, including *Les Misérables*. From 1832 to 1848, he lived on the 2nd floor of a beautiful mansion hotel that is now open to visitors. The museum-apartment retraces the author's childhood. You can see his red lounge—a sublime reception room in which he greeted guests—and the Chinese lounge that tells us about his passion for secondhand shopping and decoration. One of his custom-made writing tables (Victor Hugo wrote standing up) is still there. **Maison Victor Hugo** [6 place des Vosges, 4th] is a must-see to capture the spirit of the artist who was buried at the Pantheon in the 5th Arrondissement.

The City Hall Library

66

Who hasn't seen *Le Baiser de l'Hôtel de Ville*, photographer Robert Doisneau's famous black-and-white shot? **Hôtel de Ville** (City Hall) [5 rue de Lobau, 4th] is one of my favorite monuments in Paris. I love seeing its facades and carrousel in the sun and rain alike, its fountains in the summer and skating rink in the winter. It's like the Rockefeller Center of Paris. This place also has many secrets, including the sumptuous reception hall on the 2nd floor that was inspired by the Hall of Mirrors at Versailles. My favorite still remains the library's reading room on the 5th floor, designed by architect Édouard Deperthes in collaboration with Gustave Eiffel. His metal structure is covered in original woodwork that's listed as a historical monument.

Rue des Barres' Provincial Atmosphere

67

Steps away from the Seine, at the foot of the Saint-Gervais Gothic church, you'll find rue des Barres, a small pedestrian-only street full of charm, where I love to enjoy a quiet meal. It feels like being in a medieval village. I like taking a seat on the terrace at **L'Ébouillanté** (A) [No. 6] for a simple, sunny brunch, or head to **Chez Julien** [1 rue du Pont Louis-Philippe, 4th], a very romantic, chic bistro. The small private lounge on the second floor is perfect for a birthday or more intimate evening with friends. You can see the Île Saint-Louis from the terrace. **MIJE Fourcy** youth hostel [6 rue de Fourcy, 4th] is located in a nearby old house, a great location and perfect for modest budgets.

Sunday Brunch

68 Parisians love going for brunch. A Paris brunch consists of a plate with a series of small servings of eggs, smoked salmon, crepes, granola, salad, potatoes, bread, charcuterie, fruit... The American breakfast trend is increasingly gaining ground, and Parisians go crazy for eggs Benedict. Unfortunately, it's hard to find a really good one in Paris. That said, the creative menu and recipes at **Benedict** [19 rue Sainte-Croix-de-la-Bretonnerie, 4th] set this spot apart. They serve up all kinds of poached eggs in a lovely setting beneath a glass roof. Another great eatery to try for brunch is **Rachel's** [25 rue du Pont aux Choux, 3rd]. It opened its first restaurant after launching a pastry shop concept—and winning the prize for best cheesecake in Paris.

Spicing It Up

69 People are often critical of Parisian restaurants for lacking creativity and serving the same cuisine everywhere you go. Here's a place that's not afraid of spicing things up! **Trois Fois Plus de Piment** [84 rue Saint-Martin, 4th] allows you to choose the level of spiciness in your bowl of Szechuan noodles, on a scale of 1 to 5 (1 obviously being not spicy and 5 will turn you lobster-red and make you empty the entire water bottle!). To know which dose to go for, glance at your neighbor's face (red, blue or purple?) or ask the waiter to make a recommendation. Everything is delicious and the dumplings are homemade.

An Evening at La Mangerie

70 **La Mangerie** [7 rue de Jarente, 4th] is located on a quiet little street. Serge, the owner, will do anything to make you feel at home. Have a happy hour drink at the bar with a few tapas and take in the fabulous decor. A bike hanging on the wall, small hidden rooms... Go through the closet and you'll find yourself in another room: a garden vibe with a tree in the center and plants on the walls. They'll seat you at a large table with other diners and you can order all sorts of tapas to share. It's never a miss.

Your Dream Terrace

71 When the fair weather arrives, Parisians' endless quest to find the prettiest private terrace starts. Located in a gorgeous paved courtyard registered as a historical monument, **Grand Cœur** [41 rue du Temple, 4th] will bowl you over with its setting beneath stone arches and exposed beams. Go during the day for a quiet lunch or at night to enjoy an excellent, candle-lit tartare with fries. As romantic as you could ever hope for.

The Centre Pompidou's Red Elevator

72 If you like museums, films and exhibits, the modern, colorful Centre Pompidou is obviously a must. This place has one of the three largest collections of modern and contemporary art in the world, along with the Museum of Modern Art in New York and the Tate Modern in London. You have to pay at the main entrance, which gives you access to all the exhibitions. To go to new heights, I love taking the red elevator that leads to **Georges** [6th floor, Palais Beaubourg, Place Georges Pompidou, 4th], the restaurant at the very top. This place has a unique design, and a beautiful rose sits at each table. It's by far one of the largest rooftop terraces in Paris. From there, you can catch a panoramic view of the Eiffel Tower, all the way to Sacré-Cœur, Opéra Garnier and Notre-Dame de Paris.

Good Outlets

73 In Paris, it's always best to buy items that are on sale or from Stock boutiques that sell at marked-down prices. A must in the rocker-romantic Parisian fashion world, **Stock Sandro** [26 rue de Sévigné, 4th]—in the heart of the Marais—posts sales of up to 40 percent on current collections and previous seasons. In the area, you'll also find **Stocks Azzedine Alaïa** [18 rue de la Verrerie, 4th], the king of sexy threads beloved by celebrities. **Stock Zadig & Voltaire** [22 rue du Bourg Tibourg, 4th] is also close by and perfect for getting your hands on a cute bag or leather jacket on sale from the rocker-chic brand that Parisian women are crazy about.

Hôtel-Dieu Garden

74

In the heart of Île de la Cité, right by Cathédrale Notre-Dame de Paris—very touristy and always busy—you'll find a lovely garden in the **Hôtel-Dieu** courtyard [1 Parvis Notre-Dame–Place Jean-Paul II, 4th]. The name Hôtel-Dieu refers to the oldest hospitals in the francophone world. The garden is a good spot to find some peace in the middle of the capital. It's also the entrance to **Hôtel Hospitel** located on the 6th floor of the hospital. There are 14 simple and comfortable, reasonably priced rooms, a few of which have a view of Notre-Dame de Paris.

The Prettiest View of Île Saint-Louis

75

Place Louis Aragon [Quai de Bourbon, 4th], located at the end of the island on the Quai de Bourbon side, is a less touristy spot visited by the residents of Île Saint-Louis. Entirely paved, it has a few benches where you can relax beneath the trees, on the banks of the Seine. A few lines are written on one of the street's plaques: "Do you know the island/In the heart of town/Where all is quiet/Forever."

"To stray is human. To saunter is Parisian."
Victor Hugo

The Poets' Passageway

76 Located in the Quartier de l'Horloge, the **Passage Molière** maintains a very poetic feel. Tiny, it's nicknamed the *passage de l'encre* (ink passage). It's also home to the Maison de la Poésie and the Théâtre Molière. There are two performance halls and a beautiful Italian-style theater. They're also interested in living poets, which is rare. You can enter at rue Saint-Martin [No. 157] or rue Quincampoix [No. 82].

A Provençal Terrace

77 Right by Place des Vosges, on a street where you never would have thought to set foot, bistro **Chez Janou** [2 rue Roger Verlomme, 3rd] feels like it's straight out of a village in the South of France and is one of the most charming destinations in the Marais. No cars (in fact, your taxi will probably get lost!), almost no passersby and no reservations on the terrace (obviously), but you can have a drink at the inside bar as you wait to enjoy Provençal tuna or pistou sea bass.

78

The Secret Rose Garden

78 **Square Saint-Gilles Grand Veneur** [rue de Hesse, 3rd] is a small hidden treasure. The first time I went, I stumbled upon it by chance, lost in the Marais' maze-like alleyways. I magically fell under the spell of the countless types of roses and lawns hidden beneath rosebush archways. There are also a few benches, where locals sit to read quietly or have a picnic. You're both at the center of things and away from it all. This is where the famous Catherine Deneuve rose flowers bloom, and you can see the pretty facade of Hôtel d'Ecquevilly that was built in 1637.

The Best Galette

79 Breizh has become a galette (buckwheat pancake) institution in France and Japan. What's the link between the two? A beautiful love story: the owner Bertrand married a Japanese woman. They moved to Tokyo together before coming back to Paris and opening the **Breizh Café** [111 rue Vieille du Temple, 3rd] that showcases their know-how in the Breton crepe department, with a wonderful Tokyo twist. Come try a delicious buckwheat galette stuffed with spinach, a sunny-side up egg and grated cheese. Finish off the meal with a butter-sugar crepe, a lemon crepe and a glass of cider.

5th and 13th Arrondissements

—»»»» ★ «««—

THE
PANTHÉON
and
PARIS CHINATOWN

Explore the lower portion of rue Mouffetard,
unwind in the Arènes de Lutèce built by the ancient
Romans, descend into the Panthéon's crypt,
rejuvenate yourself surrounded by hundred-year-
old trees in Jardin des Plantes, enjoy authentic phô
in Chinatown, and dance on a rooftop under the
open sky at the Quai d'Austerlitz.

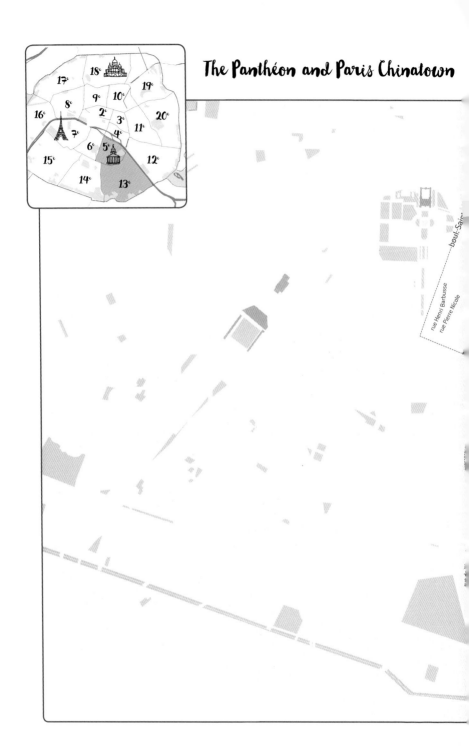

17ᵉ
18ᵉ
19ᵉ
9ᵉ
10ᵉ
8ᵉ
16ᵉ
2ᵉ
20ᵉ
3ᵉ
7ᵉ
11ᵉ
4ᵉ
6ᵉ
5ᵉ
15ᵉ
12ᵉ
14ᵉ
13ᵉ

boul.-Sain

rue Henri Barbusse
rue Pierre Nicole

89 · 88
86 ·
in du
ée Cluny
35
petit pont
rue Lagrange
pont de l'Archevêché
quai de la Tournelle
pont de la Tournelle
boul. Saint-Germain
rue Saint-Jacques
rue des Ecoles
rue du Cardinal Lemoine
rue Monge
quai Saint-Bernard
ujas pl. du Panthéon
rue Clovis
airie
87 rue Clotilde
rue Thouin · 80A
rue Rollin · 81
rue Linné
rue Cuvier
rue d'Ulm
rue Lhomond
rue Lacépède
· 81A
83
rue Mouffetard
rue Monge
82 · rue Geoffroy Saint-Hilaire
· rue Georges Desplas
rue Buffon
pl. Valhubert
e Lampué
rue Claude Bernard
80
· rue Censier
rue de Mirbel
rue Poliveau
pont Ch. de Gaulle
84 ·
rue Broca
rue Pascal
rue Scipion
boul. Saint-Marcel
boul. de l'Hôpital
quai d'Austerlitz
pont de Bercy
Port-Royal
av. des Gobelins
rue Dumeril
quai de la Gare
rue Saint-Hippolyte
rue du Banquier
rue Jenner
rue Bruant
quai François Mauriac
Arago
rue de la Glacière
rue Rubens
rue Esquirol
rue Pinel
boul. Vincent Auriol
rue du Chevaleret
pont de Tolbiac
av. de France
square René Le Gall
Mairie
av. de la Sœur Rosalie
rue Dunois
rue Jeanne d'Arc
rue Charcot
quai Panhard et Levassor
uste Blanqui
rue Corvisart
av. Edison
rue Nationale
pl. Nationale
rue de Patay
rue de Tolbiac
rue du Chevaleret
rue Olivier Messiaen
93A · rue des 5 Diamants
rue Barrault
rue Bobillot
rue Baudricourt
rue de Tolbiac
rue Albert
rue Vergniaud
av. d'Italie
impasse Baudricourt
rue du Château des Rentiers
boul. Masséna
olbiac
93
rue de l'Espérance
av. de Choisy
90
rue Régnault
rue Bobillot
rue de Tolbiac
rue Damesme
rue Nationale
av. d'Ivry
av. Boutroux
pl. de l'Abbé Georges Hénocque
rue du Moulin de la Pointe
90A
pl. de Rungis
rue du Tage
rue Caillaux
rue Philibert Lucot
pl. de Vénétie
pl. du Docteur Yersin
rue des Longues Raies
91A ·
92 ·
boul. Masséna
rue André Voguet
boul. Kellermann
jardin du Moulin de la Pointe
av. de Caffién
Poterne des Peupliers
Parc Kellermann
boul. Hipp. Marques
91 ·
av. Léon Bollée
rue du Val-de-Marne

Mouffetard Takeout

80 Rue Mouffetard, one of Paris' oldest streets, dates back to the Roman era. It's a rather touristy area that also has a very youthful spirit, being right by the Sorbonne University. At night the atmosphere is festive and very lively. Start your visit on lower Mouffetard at Place Saint-Médard. Take a break at **Café Saint Médard** [53 rue Censier, 5th]—the local hangout—before walking down the surprisingly steep pedestrian walkway, rue Mouffetard. Buy an incredible mille-feuille from **Carl Marletti** [51 rue Censier, 5th], the former pastry chef at Place de l'Opéra's famous Café de la Paix, or make like a regular and stop in at small takeout counters. You can order delicious sweet or savory crepes at **Oroyona** [No. 36] where the prices are unbeatable. Right across the street, you'll find **Dose** [No. 73], a new "coffee dealer"

concept with a second location in the Batignolles area. Order takeout coffee, juice or a snack from the small street-facing window or grab a seat on the terrace located in the adjacent passageway. At the very top of the street, you'll come across the well-known **Place de la Contrescarpe** that's lined with cafés, bars, trees and fountains. This is the epicenter of the 5th Arrondissement. Right behind the Place, you'll find **Bonjour Vietnam** (A) [6 rue Thouin, 5th], the best Vietnamese spot in Contrescarpe. You need to plan ahead to get a seat, but you'll feel right at home. Take your time, relish the fact that everything is fresh and lovingly prepared on the premises, including the traditional beef and noodle phô soup, green mango salad with crab or green papaya salad with shrimp.

Arènes de Lutèce's Alcoves

81 This is probably one of the most unusual places in town. Built in the 1st century, the Gallo-Roman amphitheater **Arènes de Lutèce** [49 rue Monge, 5th] once hosted plays and gladiator battles. Now, people come to play soccer, wander around with their kids or, better yet, curl up with a lover in one of the stone alcoves to enjoy the sunshine. Most Parisians have never set foot here. Walk among the open-air ruins: It's free and the perfect spot for an absolutely wonderful picnic. At the exit, you'll see the gorgeous blue facade of the **Paris Jazz Corner** (A) [5 rue de Navarre, 5th], one of France's best record stores for vinyl and jazz lovers.

The Grande Mosquée

82 If you're near the Panthéon and Arènes de Lutèce, take a small detour (five minutes on foot) to visit the **Grande Mosquée** [2 bis Place du Puits de l'Ermite, 5th]. It's a unique place, a soulful trip, and a treasure to discover. For €1, head straight into the heart of Hispanic-Moorish art by visiting the gardens and prayer rooms at this place of worship. I love going for the hammam or, during the summer, to enjoy an Eastern experience: a cup of tea and pastry at a table covered in blue mosaic, next to a fountain.

Jardin des Plantes

83 To get away from noisy cars, I often hide in this nature escape. Enter **Jardin des Plantes** by the Muséum National d'Histoire Naturelle doorway [57 rue Cuvier, 5th]. Just inside you can admire the *Platanus hispanica* that was planted by the naturalist Comte de Buffon in 1785. Its presence is so powerful that passersby stop to touch it and absorb its ageless energy. Marvel at the Cedar of Lebanon planted by botanist Bernard de Jussieu in 1734. Try to set aside enough time to visit the large greenhouses, menagerie and mineralogy and geology gallery, which has one of the most impressive collections in the world. Walk along the flower-lined paths that bloom throughout the seasons. You'll often see outdoor photography exhibits on the theme of Man and Nature.

Neo-Austerlitz

84 Right across from Jardin des Plantes are the **Quai** and **Gare d'Austerlitz**. For me, this aerial Metro station evokes more industrial Paris. Visit the nearby **Cité de la Mode et du Design** [34 quai d'Austerlitz, 13th], which is where many fashion shows take place during Paris Fashion Week. There are several hip restaurants inside, including **M.O.B.**, a vegan fast-food eatery that makes meat-free burgers. Everything is organic and their motto is "Be good to yourself by being good to the planet." It has an unusual decor in an industrial loft setting with a view of the Seine. A party place under the stars, **Nüba** (A) is a nightclub located on the Cité de la Mode's rooftop. This place's signature contemporary green relief structure lights up at night, and the huge terrace is often packed. The atmosphere is very festive, thanks to live bands, a canteen and everything you need for a *fiesta*.

84A

The Lady and the Unicorn

85 If the Louvre Museum has the Mona Lisa, the **Musée de Cluny** [6 Place Paul Painlevé, 5th] has its Lady and the Unicorn. Made up of six tapestries that date back to the year 1500, this masterpiece represents a reflection on the pleasures provided by the five senses and on the concept of free will. Should we be slaves to sensory, ephemeral pleasures or try to attain the purity of the unicorn (a symbol of Christ), the sword of God and divine revelation? The soothing darkness preserves the tapestries' fabulous colors.

Rasa Yoga

86 This is my favorite yoga studio [21 rue Saint-Jacques, 5th] in Paris. Right by Cathédrale Notre-Dame, in the heart of the Quartier Latin, open the door and walk to the back of the courtyard. Inside, there's a Zen atmosphere, some clothing, yoga mats, stones and inspirational reading.
The studio has two rooms, including one beneath a gorgeous glass roof. They organize workshops with teachers from around the world on a regular basis. *Namaste.*

Soufflot's Soul

87 The **Panthéon** (A)—a majestic monument dedicated to France's Greats—takes center stage at the top of Montagne Sainte-Geneviève, right by the Sorbonne. This powerful place, designed by architect Jacques-Germain Soufflot, boasts an impressive, breathtaking dome. There's a spectacular crypt in the basement: a maze of galleries where you'll find the tombs of great men of letters, such as Victor Hugo, Voltaire, René Descartes and Jean-Jacques Rousseau. For a bite to eat in these parts, head to **Café Soufflot** [16 rue Soufflot, 5th], a spot known for excellent tartare, or try **Little Cantine** [51 rue des Écoles, 5th] for delicious homemade burgers with vegetarian options. For a change of pace, **De Clercq, Les Rois de la Frite** [184 rue Saint-Jacques, 5th] is a true Belgian institution where students abound. Here, you'll sink your teeth into the freshest fries, traditionally prepared. For a romantic meal of authentic, old-style French cuisine, go to **Le Coupe-Chou** [11 rue de Lanneau, 5th], an excellent spot with a summertime terrace. The room in the basement has a wonderful fireplace that's perfect for winter evenings.

87 A

Choux Pastries Facing Notre-Dame

88 **Odette Paris** [77 rue Galande, 5th] is a favorite; it's a tiny counter where you can enjoy delicious cream-filled choux pastries. At first, you might not think you can eat on the premises, but surprise! There are a few set tables on the 1st floor in a tiny, charming space. Take a seat by the window that looks out onto Cathédrale Notre-Dame and enjoy the selection (vanilla, chocolate, pistachio, coffee, green tea, salted butter caramel, lemon, field berry or praline choux). Good to know: Frédéric Berthy opened a second shop in the 1st Arrondissement [8 rue Montorgueil, 1st]. How fun!

Paris' Oldest Tree

89 **Square René Viviani-Montebello** is a small garden that has preserved its peacefulness despite having very touristy surroundings. I love going there to re-energize after crossing Île de la Cité and Notre-Dame's crowded square. This is where you'll find Paris' oldest tree, a black locust from North America planted in 1601 by Jean Robin, the king's botanist, arborist and director of Jardin des Apothicaires. If you need some cosmic reading, the wonderful esoteric bookstore **Gibert Jeune** [23 quai Saint-Michel, 5th] stands right next door. They carry tarot cards, mystical writings and a vast, absolutely incredible selection of self-help books.

A Stroll Through Chinatown

90 In the middle of the 13th Arrondissement, you can discover the continent of Asia, a phô soup and sticky rice paradise. Very few Parisians come all the way out here and that's a real shame, since the neighborhood provides a unique experience that's a far cry from tartare and fries. Discover another Paris that's just as magical. It's named Triangle de Choisy (Choisy Triangle) and is delimited by Boulevard Masséna, Avenue de Choisy and Avenue d'Ivry. Aside from Belleville and Little Japan, this area is home to some of the capital's largest Chinese, Vietnamese, Cambodian and Laotian communities. It's also worth the trip for its Buddhist temples and wonderful, authentic Asian restaurants. Get off at Tolbiac Metro and eat at **Lao Lane Xang 2** [102 Avenue d'Ivry, 13th] to enjoy exquisite Laotian, Thai and Vietnamese homemade dishes in a chicer atmosphere. For authentic phô and a pretension-free decor, head to **Phô 18** (A) [18 rue Philibert Lucot, 13th]. Patrick Tan is Cambodian and his wife is Vietnamese, and they have run this restaurant together for six years. Phô is their specialty, the secret of which is obviously the broth concocted by the owner himself. This is where I learned to eat phô like a Vietnamese. They also explained the herbs' roles to me: Mint is meant to soothe your throat during winter and basil has refreshing properties for summer.

The Bièvre's Course

91

The Bièvre once flowed into the Seine around Gare d'Austerlitz. This Old Paris river that once ran through the 13th and 5th Arrondissements is now entirely covered. A few historic traces remain and can be discovered in the 13th Arrondissement. The sublime, but little-known **Parc Kellermann** was inaugurated in 1937 on the site of Paris' old fortifications, on what was the Bièvre riverbed. This park is full of history, complemented by pretty walkways, a large basin and a waterfall. Nearby, **Jardin du Moulin-de-la-Pointe** (A) reminds us that there used to be watermills in the Bièvre Valley. Here you can track the course of the old river by the medallions embedded in the sidewalk and bearing inscriptions "ancien lit de la Bièvre (Bièvre's old riverbed)," "bras mort (dead arm)," "bras vif (riverbed)," "bras unique (single arm)"... Just like real treasure hunt!

91A

92A 92

Open-Air Frescoes

92 The 13th Arrondissement is a gold mine for street art lovers. Look up toward the sky at a street corner and you'll see some amazing works of art on building walls. This is the Galerie Itinerrance's Street Art 13 project, a street art circuit that allows you to discover another side of the 13th Arrondissement. In total, 16 street artists of 10 different nationalities created 19 murals. My favorite is the fresco at Place de Vénétie (A) by Pantónio (Antonio Correia) that depicts a moving school of fish. It's Europe's tallest fresco.

Village Life at Butte-aux-Cailles

93 Everyone knows each other and says hello on the street here. The authentic picturesque village is preserved for tourism. Here are a few musts: **Les Cailloux** [58 rue des Cinq Diamants, 13th], a modern Italian restaurant that dominates Butte-aux-Cailles, where they filmed a few scenes from the Audrey Tautou film *Delicacy*; **Chez Gladines** (A) [30 rue des Cinq Diamants, 13th], a local legend that serves cuisine from the Southwest of France (they don't take reservations, and you might have to wait up to an hour for a table!); **Chez Mamane** [27 rue des Cinq Diamants, 13th], for its classic couscous; the homemade jewelry shop **Les Bijoux de Nico** [5 rue de la Butte aux Cailles, 13th]; the wonderful wine seller **La Cave du Moulin Vieux** [4 rue de la Butte aux Cailles]; **Place Paul Verlaine**, along rue Bobillot, for its spring water fountain and two lawn bowling courts; and rue de la Butte aux Cailles with its small bars. Among these is **Le Merle Moqueur** [No. 11], known for inexpensive (and low-quality) rums served in an enjoyable, music-filled 1980s atmosphere. Have a ball!

SAINT-GERMAIN
and
SURROUNDING AREA

Stroll through Jardin du Luxembourg, take in Place
Saint-Sulpice and Rimbaud's wall poem, stock up
on produce at the Marché Raspail organic market,
design your own custom hat at La Cerise sur
le Chapeau, meet for an afternoon drink at Café de
Flore, stop in for tapas at L'Avant Comptoir,
and end the evening at La Palette.

Saint-Germain and Surrounding Area

rue de la Santé

rue de la Santé

boul. Arago

boul. Saint-Jacques

rue du Fbg
Saint-Jacques

rue Gazan

rue d'Alésia

Cité Internationale
Universitaire
de Paris

av. Pierre de Coubertin

av. Paul Vaillant Couturier

rue Broussais

av. René Coty

120

av. Denfert-Rochereau

av. René Coty

rue de la Tombe-Issoire

rue Nansouty

119

rue David Weill

rue Schoelcher

122

rue Boulard

av. Gl. Leclerc

rue du Père Corentin

av. Reille

boul. Jourdan

av. du Docteur
Lannelongue

av. Pierre Massé

rue Froideveaux

rue Daguerre

rue Gassendi

Mairie

rue Mouton-Duvernet

pl.
Victor
Basch

rue Sarrette

rue Paul Fort

Av. du Maine

118

rue d'Alésia

rue Hippolyte Maindron

av. Jean Moulin

av. Gl. Leclerc

rue de Coulmiers

av. de la
Pte d'Orléans

rue du Château

rue Didot

rue Pernety

rue des Plantes

boul. Brune

rue Cdt. René
Mouchotte

123

rue Raymond Losserand

rue de Gergovie

av. de la Pte
de Châtillon

boul. Romain Rolland

rue de l'Ouest

rue Jacquier

rue de l'Abbé Carton

rue Didot

rue d'Alésia

av. Georges
Lafenestre

boul. Brune

boul. Adolphe Pinard

rue Vercingétorix

rue Raymond Losserand

121

pl. de
la Porte
de Vanves

boul. Brune

av. Marc Sangnier

The Juice Queen:
Claire Courtin-Clarins

94 Claire Courtin-Clarins is aptly named: She embodies light, brightness and purity. She is the granddaughter of Clarins founder Jacques Courtin and one of the company's heiresses, along with her sister Virginie and cousins Jenna and Prisca. After returning from living in New York for a few years, she launched the C'Juice brand in December 2015. "I was very influenced by the juicing trend when I lived in New York; people talked about it everywhere. I gave into it and became completely addicted to the stuff. Upon returning to France, I realized that the fruit and vegetable-based fresh juice trend wasn't well developed. I wanted to remedy the situation by creating a simple juice bar downstairs from where I live, for my own pleasure and needs."

She opened her first shop in the heart of Saint-Germain-des-Prés on 6th Arrondissement's rue du Dragon. "I chose this arrondissement because the neighborhood didn't have a juice bar yet. Most of them are located on the other bank, notably in the Marais. As the story goes, I studied at Penninghen, right next to C'Juice, on the same street, actually! I kept such good memories from back then that, when I saw this space was for rent, I immediately contacted the agency."

In this coffee and baguette capital, is the average Parisian woman generally healthy? "Parisian women are increasingly aware of their lifestyle, especially when it comes to nutrition. I'm actually pleasantly surprised to see such movement and change on a daily basis," says the woman who tasted her first juice at age 10. "I was in Miami with my sister and father. After rollerblading on the beach, our dad took us to a juice bar. He ordered three grass juices. My sister and I hated it, but he loved it! He always imposed a very plant-based, fresh and organic diet on us, which was tied to physical activity. I hated it when I was young, but now I'm very grateful to him," she says. As for her grandfather, Jacques Courtin, he passed on his passion for plants and nature to Claire. Nowadays, her healthy juices are made with infused plants to reinvigorate skin and strengthen hair and nails.

The young woman now splits her time between London and Paris. "When I'm in Paris, I like to hang out in quintessentially Parisian spots like **Café de Flore** [172 Boulevard Saint-Germain, 6th] for a drink with friends or grab lunch at **Lipp** [151 Boulevard Saint-Germain, 6th] with my lover to marvel at the gorgeous original decor and enjoy perfect French food. As for shopping, I like going to **Céline** [16 rue de Grenelle, 6th], **Maison Margiela** [13 rue de Grenelle, 6th] or **Acne Studios** on the quays [1 quai Voltaire, 6th]. **La Hune** [16 rue de l'Abbaye, 6th], my favorite bookstore, has a very in-depth selection of architecture and design volumes."

LE BATEAU
IVRE
ARTHUR RIMBAUD

RUE FÉROU

96

Marché Bio Raspail

95 Lovers of fresh ingredients, organic free-range chicken eggs and local products should add **Marché Bio Raspail** [Boulevard Raspail, 6th] to their list. It's the largest organic market in Paris. Get off at Rennes Metro and you'll find yourself at the heart of the market on Boulevard Raspail's median strip between rue de Rennes and rue du Cherche-Midi. Get there early because the best fish goes quickly and people line up on sunny days. Prices are quite high, but quality is second to none.

Rimbaud's Wall Poem

96 In Paris' literary epicenter—on rue Férou [6th] between rue de Vaugirard and Place Saint-Sulpice—you'll see this gem: a wall completely covered by the hundred lines of poet Arthur Rimbaud's masterful work, *Bateau Ivre* ("The Drunken Boat"). Dutch painter Jan Willem Bruins wrote the lines there in calligraphy. On September 30, 1871, Rimbaud is said to have recited his poem in a restaurant at the corner of rue Bonaparte and rue du Vieux Colombier, where there is also a commemorative plaque. Dutch foundation Tegen-Beeld was behind the project and allegedly had to wait nine years to get the necessary authorization to create the piece.

95

Luxembourg's Treasures

97A

97

love strolling through **Jardin du Luxembourg** [6ᵗʰ]; it's an oasis in one of Paris' most beautiful neighborhoods. Take a seat by the central pool, facing **Palais du Luxembourg,** for a rest in the sun as you gaze upon the beautiful flower beds. Or sit in the shade of the legendary **Fontaine Médicis** (A), also known as the "Luxembourg Grotto," built in 1630 during Marie de Medici's reign. The garden is chock-full of treasures like the greenhouses that contain some 400 orchid species. In the middle of the garden is **Pavillon de la Fontaine**, a charming little restaurant with a few tables on the terrace. Marvel at the many statues of famous people, such as Beethhoven and Baudelaire. Inside **Musée du Luxembourg** [19 rue de Vaugirard, 6ᵗʰ], you'll also find a new **Angelina** branch, the legendary 1ˢᵗ Arrondissement tearoom that became famous for its incredible "Africains" hot chocolate with traditional chestnut cream Mont-Blanc. It's a good option for avoiding the interminable wait at the rue de Rivoli location, while taking in a little exhibit! You'll often see lovely open-air photo exhibits along the garden gates on rue de Vaugirard. It could take up a whole day if you let it!

À LA PARISIENNE

A word about English...

You will quickly discover how many English words and expressions are used in Paris. Contrary to what it may seem, however, these are indeed French words. Although Parisians frequently use anglicisms, to their mind they are still speaking French—*not English*. That's why they pronounce English words with a thick French accent. Say these same words with a proper English accent, and the Parisian will brand you a "tourist," and address you in English only. Since our goal is to mingle with real Parisians, do as they do: Pronounce English words with a French accent, and say "Avez-vous le we-fee (WiFi)?"

The Unfinished Tower

98 There's a special, almost mystical atmosphere at **Église Saint-Sulpice** [2 rue Palatine, 6th], the church where scenes from *The Da Vinci Code* novel unfold. Take in the building from the majestic fountain in the center of Place Saint-Sulpice. They say it took over 130 years to build it. Shorter by 5 meters (16 ½ feet), the right-hand tower was never finished due to lack of funding. The one on the left that's decorated with four statues was damaged by shellfire in 1871. Restoration lasted for more than 11 years and cost more than €28 million. The interior is also worth the trip to see the absolutely magnificent Chapelle de Saints-Anges paintings by Eugène Delacroix.

Left Bank Eating and Going Out

99 There are real Parisian gems on the small streets adjacent to Place Saint-Sulpice. Rue des Canettes [6th] is named after the sign located at No. 18 that features small, swimming ducks. Marcel Proust's servant opened **Hôtel La Perle** [No. 14] long ago, after the writer's death. On this small cobblestone street, eat at **Chez Bartolo** [No. 7], a very charming Italian eatery that makes excellent pizza in a wood-burning oven. On nearby rue Princesse, you'll find **Coffee Parisien** (A) [No. 4] that gets taken over on weekends by locals searching for eggs Benedict and American-style burgers. Enjoy excellent tapas at **La Mangerie** [No. 6]—sister restaurant of La Mangerie in the 4th Arrondissement—which is also very lively in the evening. The star on this street, however, is hidden behind a mysterious red facade: the legendary **Castel** nightclub [No. 15] where Salvador Dalí, Brigitte Bardot, Catherine Deneuve and Serge Gainsbourg partied with the Left Bank's chic bourgeoisie. Here, VIPs dance until dawn next to Gainsbourg's famous piano. If you want to get in, you absolutely need to be accompanied by a regular with a membership card in hand.

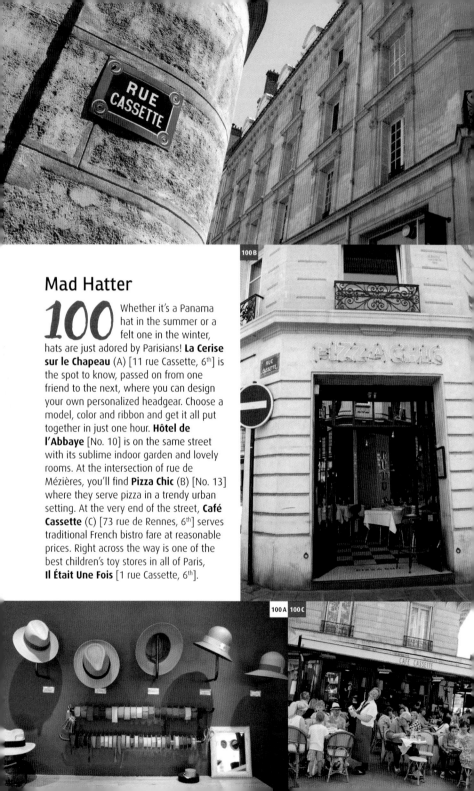

Mad Hatter

100

Whether it's a Panama hat in the summer or a felt one in the winter, hats are just adored by Parisians! **La Cerise sur le Chapeau** (A) [11 rue Cassette, 6th] is the spot to know, passed on from one friend to the next, where you can design your own personalized headgear. Choose a model, color and ribbon and get it all put together in just one hour. **Hôtel de l'Abbaye** [No. 10] is on the same street with its sublime indoor garden and lovely rooms. At the intersection of rue de Mézières, you'll find **Pizza Chic** (B) [No. 13] where they serve pizza in a trendy urban setting. At the very end of the street, **Café Cassette** (C) [73 rue de Rennes, 6th] serves traditional French bistro fare at reasonable prices. Right across the way is one of the best children's toy stores in all of Paris, **Il Était Une Fois** [1 rue Cassette, 6th].

102

Kamel Mennour's Galleries

101 The 6th arrondissement is home to art galleries that you can visit as you stroll along rue de Seine, rue Mazarine, rue Jacob, rue des Beaux-Arts... I recommend visiting **Galerie Kamel Mennour** [47 rue Saint-André-des-Arts, 6th]**, which specializes in contemporary art. Located in a gorgeous mansion hotel with a cobblestone courtyard, the gallery has pieces by some incredible artists, including Anish Kapoor, in a contemporary, airy and luminous setting beneath a glass roof. At No. 6 on rue du Pont de Lodi, the same gallery owner showcases work by Daniel Buren, who designed the Palais-Royal's famed columns.

Happy Hour by the Fireplace

102 At the very back of the 17th-century **Hôtel d'Aubusson's Café Laurent** [33 rue Dauphine, 6th], there is a timeless, quintessentially Parisian spot where I love to sip tea and work quietly. With chandeliers, original beams, an incredible stone fireplace and old French decor, it's all very chic. Order tea, take a seat in a plush armchair and enjoy the free Wi-Fi. A fire crackles in the hearth as of 6 p.m. in the winter, and they also host live jazz shows at 6.p.m., from Wednesday to Sunday. It's an excellent place to escape on a rainy day or take a romantic break.

Made-in-France Rubber

103 At **Aigle** [139 Boulevard Saint-Germain, 6th], France's "premium outdoor lifestyle brand," you'll find the coolest boot bar in Paris. They sell the nicest selection of French-made one hundred percent natural rubber rain boots. Grab a pair of Miss Juliettes, equipped with a small heel, to match the perfect style of a French woman heading to a Loire castle for a hunting weekend.

Buci Village

104 The intersection of rue de Seine and rue de Buci is one of Saint-Germain-des-Prés' epicenters. Among the institutions worth mentioning, **Bar du Marché** (A) [75 rue de Seine, 6th] is worth my noting for their unique terrace and cute overalls-donning garbed. The bistro **Père et Filles** [81 rue de Seine, 6th] is one of my favorites with an art nouveau decor, woodwork, checkered floor and lovely summertime terrace. Finish off the meal with one of **Grom**'s [81 rue de Seine, 6th] seemingly endless ice cream flavors; they're one of the best Italian gelato makers in Paris. The amazing **Taschen** bookstore [2 rue de Buci, 6th] is worth the trip for their selection of coffee table books and its Philippe Starck design. Stop in at **Allison** [3 rue de Buci, 6th], a boutique that features a selection of French brands at reasonable prices. From little cocktail dresses to casual suits, there's something for everyone. For a trendy vibe, eat at **Germain** (B) [25 rue de Buci, 6th], a restaurant that belongs to the renowned Costes brothers. The India Mahdavi-designed space features an enormous statue by contemporary art star Xavier Veilhan in the middle of the dining room. **Germain Paradisio**, the underground basement cinema is even more secret.

107 A

La Palette

105 All roads lead to **La Palette** [43 rue de Seine, 6th], the meeting spot for hip, bobo Parisians. Happy hour stretches until midnight and the vibe is festive. Given the close proximity, you'll end up talking to your neighbor, meeting new people and leaving with the friends you've made for the second half of a night of spontaneous inebriation. Many people chain-smoke throughout; It's Paris! They thankfully serve a few snacks, mixed boards and croque monsieur to share, which is necessary to soak up all that rosé wine [43 rue de Seine, 6th].

Beauty Beneath the Arches

106 Launched in 2012 by Juliette Levy, the **Oh My Cream!** concept store [3 rue de Tournon, 6th] has a personalized beauty approach. Brands like Tata Harper, Susanne Kaufmann and Antipodes are carefully curated and mostly exclusive to the store. It's a Zen space where experts dispense all kinds of tips adapted to your needs. You can get a free skin diagnosis, and there's an amazing treatment room beneath the stone archways in the basement. It's an excellent destination for a bit of relaxation and beauty pampering.

Odéon's Food Bars

107 When you exit Odéon Metro, turn left toward **L'Avant Comptoir**. Here, choose the "cochonnaille" (pork) or "mer" (seafood) side depending on your mood; both are local musts. The former food bar [9 Carrefour de l'Odéon, 6th] made its name thanks to their microscopic space and to-die-for food. Enjoy it casually, leaning against the counter with a glass of wine, delicious croquettes, codfish brandade (dip) and hot or cold dried sausage. Next door, newbie **L'Avant Comptoir de la Mer** (A) [3 Carrefour de l'Odéon, 6th] serves a range of seafood hors d'oeuvres: Spanish-style sea urchin and shrimp, roasted Coquilles Saint-Jacques, cuttlefish tagliatelle in broth and shrimp à la plancha. For an option with stools that's a notch fancier, **Etna** [33 rue Mazarine, 6th] serves small plates and biological wines. Better yet, **Freddy's** [54 rue de Seine, 6th], my fave, specializes in fine tapas: octopus salad, fish cakes in spicy green sauce *(sauce chien)* and squash with chickpeas. Get there early!

107 A

Saint-Germain's Hamptons

108
Inspired by the Ralph Lauren fashion house, **Ralph's** [173 Boulevard Saint-Germain, 6th] can lay claim to having one of the most beautiful courtyards on the Left Bank. Located in an old mansion hotel right by Odéon is this meeting spot for the Parisian elite looking for some American flavor. Decorated with couches and Hamptons-style cushions, everything is very "Ralph" and in good taste. Taste their crab cakes or one of six burgers: Ralph's Burger, Ralph's Double Burger, the Santa Fe, or turkey, red tuna or vegetarian burgers.

The Mazarine Library

109
I absolutely adore old books and the smell of their paper that's full of history. If you can visit only one library in Paris, it should be **Bibliothèque Mazarine** [23 quai de Conti, 6th], the oldest in France. The reading room has 140 seats and was entirely restored in an authentic 17th-century style. The space itself tells a story before you've had a chance to read a single line from one of the 600,000 documents it contains—truly staggering riches.

Lapérouse's Private Lounges

110
Established in 1766, this old mansion hotel, turned into a restaurant and bar decorated with original frescoes and woodwork, is a Parisian legend. Crowds and paparazzi gather here, hoping to catch a glimpse of celebrities hidden in the private lounges that can be reserved for a meal away from prying eyes. As the story goes, mistresses of very rich men used their rings to scratch the mirrors in certain lounges. Guy de Maupassant, Émile Zola, Alexandre Dumas and Victor Hugo—one of the lounges' namesakes—spent time at **Lapérouse** [51 quai des Grands Augustins, 6th].

Oscar Wilde's Room

111

This is Paris' smallest five-star hotel. It has 20 rooms and was Oscar Wilde's final home. He lived here from 1898 until his death in 1900 in room No. 16 that is maintained in the era's Victorian style. In the 1960s, **L'Hôtel** [13 rue des Beaux-Arts, 6th] was a chic spot visited by artists, stars and hip Parisians. Even if you don't stay at the hotel, eat at their restaurant called **Le Restaurant** (with one Michelin star) or have a drink at **Le Bar**. This place is worth a detour for the incredible six-floor, circular stairway that goes all the way up to the cupola. Let's not forget the underground pool beneath archways, which is reserved for hotel guests.

Pushkin's Café

112

Boulevard Saint-Germain, where you'll find legendary cafés like **Flore** and **Les Deux Magots** [6 Place Saint-Germain des Près, 6th], is home to a new, unusual destination: **Café Pouchkine** [155 Boulevard Saint-Germain, 6th], also has locations at Printemps Haussmann [64 Boulevard Haussmann, 9th] and Place des Vosges [2 rue des Francs Bourgeois, 3rd]. This café brings Russian splendor back to life, serving many pastries, including the famous *medovick* (a honey-flavored buckwheat cookie made up of many thin layers), *sgouchonka* (milk spread) and *smetana* (slightly sour fresh cream). Enjoy them indoors or on the terrace with a view of the lovely Abbaye de Saint-Germain-des-Prés.

Le Flore

113

It's impossible to not mention **Café de Flore** [172 Boulevard Saint-Germain, 6th], the legendary place that remains a real local institution for Parisians in spite of all the tourists. Lengthy discussions take place here at all hours of the day. If you're lucky enough to grab a table on the terrace, you might see Karl Lagerfeld, singer David Hallyday or model and entrepreneur Inès de La Fressange who lives in the neighborhood. She's also a regular at **L'Écumes des Pages** bookstore next door [No. 174] where she occasionally signs her latest book, *Mon Paris* ("My Paris").

115

Tea Ceremonies

114

The first **Jugetsudo** Japanese teahouse [95 rue de Seine, 6th] opened its doors in Tokyo in 2003. The owners chose Saint-Germain-des-Prés as the location for their second shop. If you're a green tea lover, this place, designed with the utmost respect for Japanese tradition, was made for you. The shop has a retail space and tasting room decorated with hanging bamboo stalks. Customers are, however, unaware of the room beneath the arches where masters host tea ceremony initiations. It's fascinating.

The Best Maki

115

In Paris, sushi is rather traditional and devoid of creativity. It's a far cry from the incredible variety available in Canada and the United States, but **Blueberry** [6 rue du Sabot, 6th] is an exception. Colorful: the word sums up the atmosphere at this restaurant that specializes in creative maki. Try the Rackham le Rouge maki (tempura shrimp, black truffle, marinated tuna, cucumber, spicy mayonnaise, chive and flying fish eggs) or Little Miss Yuzu (yuzu-marinated salmon tataki, raspberry, fresh mango and Thai chives). For dessert, the amazing iced mochi (bean paste green tea ice cream) is delicious, with flavors like cherry blossom, green tea and sesame.

À LA PARISIENNE

Under scrutiny

Parisians have an opinion about everything—especially you! Your weight, your skin, your job, your romantic life. If you aren't willing to set aside your ego and open yourself up to this personal scrutiny, you will never have good relationships—or "bonnes relations," as they say. In Paris, your appearance is everyone's business.

A Literary Triangle

116 The Saint-Germain neighborhood is known as the home of intellectual authors, great spirits and masters of words and thought. A stop at **Les Éditeurs** [4 Carrefour de l'Odéon, 6th] is in order. This library-restaurant is across the street from **Hibou** [No. 16], a great two-story bistro with a lovely terrace. Just a bit farther east, take rue Monsieur le Prince and follow the small neighborhood bookstore circuit, some of which specialize in old books with rare bindings. At the very end of the street, **Polidor** [No. 41] is one of the oldest bistros in Paris and its facade remains unchanged. Many famous artists have been here, including René Clair, Paul Valéry, Boris Vian and Ernest Hemingway. Good to know: The street is also home to an excellent Italian eatery, **Luisa Maria** [No. 12].

The Smallest Door

117 Your have to have a supple back to be able to get through the entrance to **Shu** [8 rue Suger, 6th], an excellent Japanese restaurant in the heart of Odéon. The door is barely one meter high (3.3 feet), but once you're on the other side, go down a few steps and you'll find yourself in a timeless spot. Take a seat at the counter to enjoy one of three tasting menus (suzu, kyôu or kazé) that include appetizers, sashimi, kushiage (battered skewers) and miso soup. Watch the chef at work behind the counter; it's the perfect destination to impress people and spend a unique evening.

Rue du Château's Neo-Bistros

118 Perpendicular to rue Raymond Losserand—the neighborhood's nicest commercial street—you'll find the small rue du Château, the 14th Arrondissement's bistronomy hot spot. Get a table at **Nina** [No. 139], a counter-style restaurant that's youthful and creative. Try the generous portion of amazing grilled Wagyu beef or, for smaller appetites, the "mosaic" version (tasting portion). **Kigawa** [No. 186] is a refined neo-bistro with about 20 seats where you'll eat delicious French cuisine, regularly reinvented based on what's fresh at the market. **L'Assiette** (A) [No. 181] remains the street's star restaurant. Located in an old charcuterie shop, this establishment is very well known among Parisians and once belonged to Lucette Rousseau, the charming owner who goes by Lulu and put the neighborhood on the map. People say that former French President François Mitterrand ate at table No. 4 each week, while Catherine Deveuve and Pierre Bergé preferred No. 15. Nowadays, chef David Rathgeber runs the place. The clientele is younger, but the atmosphere is still just as welcoming. Who knows, you could cross paths with Marion Cotillard.

"The real Parisian does not like Paris, but cannot live anywhere else."

Alphonse Karr

L'Assiette

On peut APPORTER son MANGER

PLAT du JOUR

Montsouris Square

119 Parc Montsouris is without a doubt the one that has kept the most authentic wild soul with its diverse fauna and wide variety of insects and birds to show for it. You can visit **Square Montsouris** [14th] nearby, a wonderful and unusual cobblestone alleyway, where you'll see 62 Art Nouveau and Art Deco villas that were built in the early 1920s. The walkway lined with lush vegetation was once a part of the old Quartier du Petit-Montrouge that was annexed from Paris in 1860. The square was registered in 1975 to preserve the space.

Vanves' Flea Markets

121 Let yourself be tempted by the old jewelry, trinkets, paintings, drawings, engravings and the endless variety of antiques you'll find here every Saturday and Sunday of the year. **Puces de Vanves** [Métro Porte de Vanves, 14th] strives to be a trip to the heart of the 18th and 19th centuries. It's also home to many objects from the 1950s and 1970s. You can find really great deals! The market takes up two streets: avenue Marc Sangnier from 7 a.m. to 1 p.m. and avenue Georges Lafenestre from 7 a.m. to 5 p.m.

The International Park

120 Parc de la Cité Internationale Universitaire [17 Boulevard Jourdan, 14th] is managed according to sustainable development criteria and is the third largest in Paris. Thirteen gardeners maintain the land, doing all the weeding with steam or by hand. The park overlooks the impressive **Maison Internationale** whose architecture is inspired from Château de Fontainebleau: an ideal place to go green. You might cross paths with students of 141 different nationalities.

The Fondation Cartier Garden

122 Established in 1984 by Alain-Dominique Perrin, who was then the president of Cartier International, **Fondation Cartier** [261 Boulevard Raspail, 14th] is a Left Bank cornerstone of contemporary art. You can catch exhibits, major retrospectives and photographs presented in a unique, modern space flooded with sublime light, thanks to the metal and glass design by architect Jean Nouvel. My absolute fave is *Theatrum Botanicum* by Lothar Baumgarten, the name of which was inspired by the books in which monks kept an inventory of medicinal plants and herbs during the Middle Ages. It's a wild place enclosed by an ancient wall where nature is reclaiming its space, once inhabited by Chateaubriand.

"Whoever does not visit Paris regularly will never truly be elegant."

Honoré de Balzac

Fabrice Midal
Practicing the essence of meditation

123 Fabrice Midal is one of the main proponents of meditation in France. He has published over 40 books because, as he puts it, he has "something to say." His biography of *Chögyam Trungpa* has been translated into English. He gives conferences and workshops free of charge every Wednesday at l'**École Occidentale de Méditation** [53 rue Raymond Losserand, 14th] to help demystify meditation.

"I don't just try to tell people what they need, I try to talk to them to create real change. I want to touch them deeply. That's very different from attempting to meet people's needs, which is more of a marketing approach. I try to convey the most simple and profound dimension of meditation," he says.

A pioneer of meditation in France, he is now attempting, in response to growing enthusiasm for this lifestyle practice, to preserve the authenticity of its origins. "My intention is to denounce meditation as a tool for enhancing performance or for stress management. That's a social ruse, and it's completely barbaric. Meditation must, above all, retain an ethical dimension and lead to a deep compassion toward ourselves and the world." In addition to his publishing and teaching work, he collaborates with physicians to help them in their work, and also advises teachers on teaching meditation to children. "We have seen that it does help people, as long as you are sure to preserve its ethical and compassionate elements."

What does he believe are the benefits of meditation? "If meditation has a purpose, it is to liberate us from our obsession with control. To make peace with the self, to have compassion for our own pain, to develop a sense of presence, of kindness. We make peace, we stop blaming ourselves for being too sensitive and develop more confidence. This allows us to stop apologizing for not being perfect. We find the ability to be kind to ourselves, and to free ourselves from guilt."

In his classes, he teaches people to be in the moment, plain and simple. "Meditation is re-learning something very simple—a sense of presence. It's a way to be in tune with your body, your heart. We don't close our eyes, and we don't do the lotus. It's as simple as that, but it transforms everything. We stop wanting to understand. Forget peace. We are elsewhere. There is no strategy, period. We go back to being human beings, and allow ourselves to simply be."

Midal is a book lover who adores Parisian bookshops. His favorites? "Librairie **Gibert Joseph** at Saint-Germain-des-Prés [26 boulevard Saint-Michel, 6th], which is great and is on three floors. It also sells used books. I can find all the old books I want. I love it. And for the truly esoteric and mystical, **Gibert Jeune** [23 quai Saint-Michel, 5th]."

7th and 15th Arrondissements

IN THE
Shadow of the
EIFFEL TOWER

Lounge in the deck chairs along the Seine, revel in the secret garden at the Musée Rodin, marvel at the golden Dôme des Invalides, stroll down rue Cler, cross Pont de Bir-Hakeim in the elevated Metro, and discover the futurist design of Beaugrenelle and Parc André-Citroën.

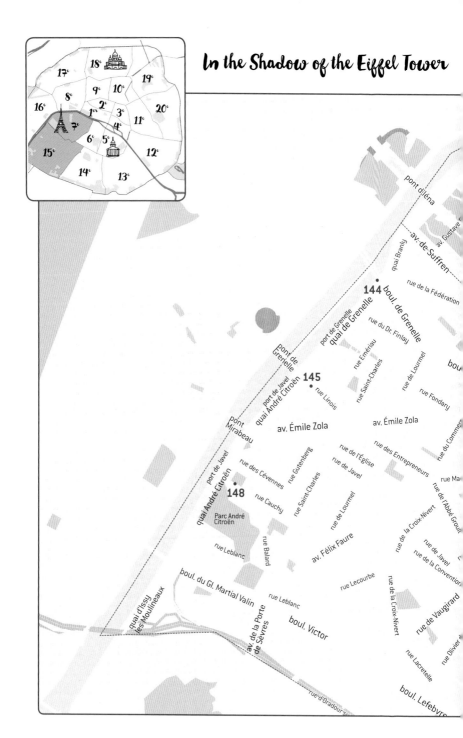

pont des Invalides

pont de l'Alma

port du Gros Caillou

quai d'Orsay

pont Alexandre

138

port des Invalides

port de la Concorde

quai Anatole France

pont du Carrousel

31

av. Rapp

av. Bosquet

rue Sédillot

rue Malar

rue Jean Nicot

rue Fabert

rue de l'Université

rue Saint-Dominique

rue de Lille

boul. Saint-Germain

rue Las Cases

130

rue de Verneuil

126

rue de l'Université

143

rue du Bac

rue des Saint-Pères

137

136

135

rue Cler

rue de la Comète

quai d'Orsay

132

rue de Grenelle

133

rue Duvivier

boul. de la Tour-Maubourg

139

rue de Bourgogne

127

128

Mairie

rue de Bellechasse

rue de Grenelle

boul. Saint-Germain

140

av. de La Bourdonnais

boul. des Invalides

Constantine

rue de Tourville

129

rue Barbet de Jouy

rue de Varenne

141

boul. Raspail

125

av. de La Motte-Picquet

av. Duquesne

av. de Tourville

rue de Babylone

124

les Floquet

illage uisse

rue du Laos

av. de Lowendal

av. de Ségur

av. de Saxe

boul. des Invalides

134

rue Oudinot

rue Vaneau

rue Vaneau

rue de Sèvres

elle

micourt

Croix-Nivert

av. de Suffren

142

rue Pérignon

rue Bouchut

av. de Breteuil

boul. Garibaldi

boul.-du-Montparnasse

rue Cambronne

rue Clouet

rue Lecourbe

rue Falguière

rue de Vaugirard

boul. Pasteur

boul. de Vaugirard

147

rue Blomet

rue des Volontaires

rue du Dr. Roux

rue Falguière

rue Bargue

Mairie

rue du Gl. Beuret

rue Paul Barruel

rue de l'Abbé Groult

rue de la Procession

s Morillons

rue de Cronstadt

rue Brancion

rue de Vouillé

rue Labrouste

rue Castagnary

16 Parc Georges Brassens

Shoe Shopping at Bon Marché

124

Le Bon Marché is one of Paris' finest shopping malls and was the city's first department store when it opened in 1852. This place is legendary for its beauty department, art deco escalator and large grocery store where you'll find an amazing selection of fine products. The best reason to head over, however, is the shoe area, established in a kind of amphitheater beneath a glass roof. It's a temptation-filled destination where you'll discover creations by the greatest designers (Chloé, Dries Van Noten, Givenchy, Jil Sander, Lanvin, Marni, Proenza Schouler, etc.). While you're there, stop in at Rose Bakery Tea Room for freshly pressed juice and an extra-large piece of lemon pie [24 rue de Sèvres, 7ᵗʰ].

À LA PARISIENNE

The Other Side of Light

Of all the capital cities in the world, Paris is the most adept at promoting its own image. Everywhere you go, you'll see signs proclaiming: Paris, the city of love; of celebration; of magic. Paris, City of Light! And it's true—there's magic everywhere, and beauty and love abound. It's safe to say that people dream of Paris even when they live there. But beyond the enchantment, Paris can also be dangerous at times. Pickpockets are common, and some Metro lines are less safe than others, so make sure to be vigilant, without becoming paranoid. If you go to the 7th arrondissement, for example, avoid line 13, which is not too secure, and watch your bag at all times. You know you're one hundred percent Parisian when your vociferous mistrust of Paris is energetically matched by your conviction that it is the most beautiful city in the world.

Erwin Creed
The seventh heir

125 Erwin Creed is the 7th heir of the Creed family, a fragrance dynasty whose history dates back to 1760. Their perfumes are a huge success around the world and their story is an inspirational one. In the 18th century, James Henry Creed was a clothing merchant and official supplier to the British Court and Queen Victoria. He sold dresses, fabrics and gloves, as well as very strong perfumes that were applied in small amounts behind the ear. In 1854, at the request of Empress Eugénie, wife of Napoleon III, Henry Creed opened his first shop on rue Royale, in Paris, where he made custom clothing. Following in the footsteps of his forebears, Olivier Creed—the current CEO—reintroduced perfume in 1970. He closed the shop on rue Royale and opened a boutique at 38 Avenue Pierre 1er de Serbie. At the back of the boutique is a selection of shirts, ties and sweaters, a legacy from their origins in the tailoring business. In 2012, Creed Parfumerie opened a second boutique [74 rue des Saints-Pères, 7th].

Today, Erwin Creedand his sister Olivia are worthy heirs of the family tradition.

Among the Maison Creed's most successful creations is Fleurissimo, which was ordered especially by Monaco's Prince Rainier for his marriage to Grace Kelly in 1956. It contains ylang-ylang, tuberose and Bulgarian rose. Kate Middleton also chose the scent for her wedding. "I love it. It's very floral, round, and focused on heart notes. It's a lovely, classic perfume that brings out the intoxicating element of the flower," explained Erwin, who also had a hand in creating Original Vétiver, Love in White, Original Santal, Feuille Verte, Royal Ceylan, Fleurs de Gardenia, Virgin Island Water, Acqua Fiorentina and Aventus.

So what is life like for the 7th heir of the Maison Creed? "I live in Paris and Geneva, and travel the world to discover everything that goes into making perfume." Does he have a favorite childhood memory? "When I was seven, my father had a laboratory in our country house. I was having trouble sleeping one night, so I went to see him, and we created a perfume together, a citrus violet. We called it "Pinocchio," after our dog. That perfume doesn't exist anymore," he laughed. What's his personal signature? "I like classic perfumes. A really good bergamot, a really good lemon, peppermint... We prefer to make fewer fragrances, but of very high quality. You can smell the difference in a high quality perfume. It's less aggressive in terms of scent, and the notes are richer." His favorite spots in Paris: "Chez **David Mallett** [14 rue Notre-Dame-des-Victoires, 2nd]; my hairdresser's name is Rishi. **Le Griffonnier**, just steps from the Élysée [8 rue des Saussaies, 8th], for a typically French restaurant. And the **Acne Studios** store [124 Galerie de Valois, 1st] for jeans."

The Best Endangered Products

126 After working at Givenchy and Galeries Lafayette, entrepreneur Maud Zilnyk decided to change her life and pair up with anti-industrialization-and-globalization militant Lucio Hornero to open **Épicerie Générale** [43 rue de Verneuil, 7th], their own shop full of organic, local and fair trade products. Here, you'll find organic, French and seasonal goods. They also support products that are threatening to disappear, including cream, charcuterie, Camargue rice, regional rillettes, preserves from l'île d'Yeu and the only jambon de Paris (Parisian ham) still made in Paris. They prepare lunch menus, and you can order "super food" options, personalized according to your taste (with seasonal fruit, maca or spirulina). Their motto: Only sell products with French green label Chouette Nature's seal of approval. What's not to like?

Le Basilic

127 Le Basilic is one of my favorite spots in Paris. This brasserie is located in the shadow of the wonderful Basilique Sainte-Clotide, in a residential neighborhood right by Les Invalides. It has a lovely summertime terrace, perfect for a quiet meal. In the winter, come with friends and take a seat inside at one of the long red booths surrounded by an authentic art deco bistro decor. This place with it's laid-back atmosphere gets crowded with Paris' golden youth. The owner, Fabrice, is a local legend. Who knows, he might greet you with a smile and a glass of champagne [2 rue Casimir Périer, 7th].

India Mahdavi's Showroom

128 Paris design icon India Mahdavi has played many roles: architect, designer, stylist and even interior decorator. Known for her nomadic and minimalistic style, she decorated the rooms at Hôtel Thoumieux, and worked with the likes of Alber Elbaz (Lanvin's old artistic director), Maja Hoffman and Thierry Costes (one of the famous Costes brothers). If you're a design lover, I recommend checking out her showroom [3 rue las Cases, 7th] and small items boutique [No. 19].

The Rodin Museum Garden

129 This gem right by Les Invalides is isolated from everything else. Established in a three-hectare (7.4-acre) park, the former Hôtel Biron, an 18th-century mansion hotel, is now home to **Musée Rodin** [79 rue de Varenne, 7th]. Auguste Rodin, Jean Cocteau and Henri Matisse all had workshops here, and you can catch one of the most romantic views in town at the back of the garden. Stroll down the walkways, marvel at *La Porte de l'Enfer* (The Gates of Hell) behind the rose garden, sit by the pool in the middle of the sumptuous space surrounding you and take in the location's peacefulness. Garden access only costs €4 (€2 on Wednesdays after 6 p.m.) and is free on every first Sunday of the month, from October 1 to March 31.

True-Blue Bistro

130
Long red booths, a counter and menus written on the chalkboard: this is **Le Vin de Bellechasse** [20 rue de Bellechasse, 7th], a true-blue Parisian go-to for dinner with friends on weeknights or weekends. The clientele is young and you'll feel right at home. Share a delicious beef rib, served with the classic sides you'll find in all Parisian bistros (mashed potatoes, french fries, green beans and spinach).

Museum Rooftop Terrace

131
For a special occasion or unique time, head to **Musée du Quai Branly**'s rooftop restaurant **Les Ombres** (A) for the incredible, clear view of the Eiffel Tower. This museum is one of my favorites in Paris. It's eye-catching, thanks to an amazing plant-covered wall: The biodiverse vertical garden patented by Patrick Blanc. **Café Branly** [27 quai Branly, 7th] is a serene oasis in the middle of the museum's garden. Go there at any time of day, before or after catching an exhibit or simply to enjoy a bit of quiet in the heart of the city. Taking in an exhibit is a must.

The Best Casseroles

132
Every good, self-respecting Parisian knows about **Les Cocottes** [135 rue Saint-Dominique, 7th], the 7th Arrondissement mainstay created by Christian Constant. Enjoy their exquisite array of casserole dishes: poached eggs with lardoons, shellfish bisque, scallops, foie gras confit, etc. Good to know: The restaurant is open seven days a week and you can eat at the counter! It's an absolute must.

131A

132

Californian Hangout

133

While there are more and more healthy juice bars, it's often a challenge in Paris to break the traditional mold, to find a spot with modern decor and a healthy menu modeled on Californian eateries. I fell in love with **Marlon** [159 rue de Grenelle, 7th] with its star-bearing logo, huge bay windows, cacti, luminous space and wonderful energy. Owner Alexandra is also behind the Marcel restaurants that are very sought-after by Parisians. The menu—created by the California-loving chef—lists freshly pressed juice, tacos, ceviche, quesadillas, acai bowls and amazing grilled grapefruit for dessert.

A Rare Café

134

At **Coutume** (A) [47 rue de Babylone, 7th], coffee is elevated to specialty status. They make brews with rare roasts, as well as signature coffee cocktails concocted by a barista. Enjoy very high-quality coffee made with beans from Costa Rica, Indonesia, Brazil, Ethiopia and Burundi, all carefully selected by founders Tom Clark and Antoine Nétien. You can also take professional training classes in the roasting workshop [8 rue Martel, 10th] to learn how to make good coffee properly. Another spot, **Coutume Instituutti** [60 rue des Écoles, 5th], is right in the heart of the Institut Culturel Finlandais (Finland Cultural Institute).

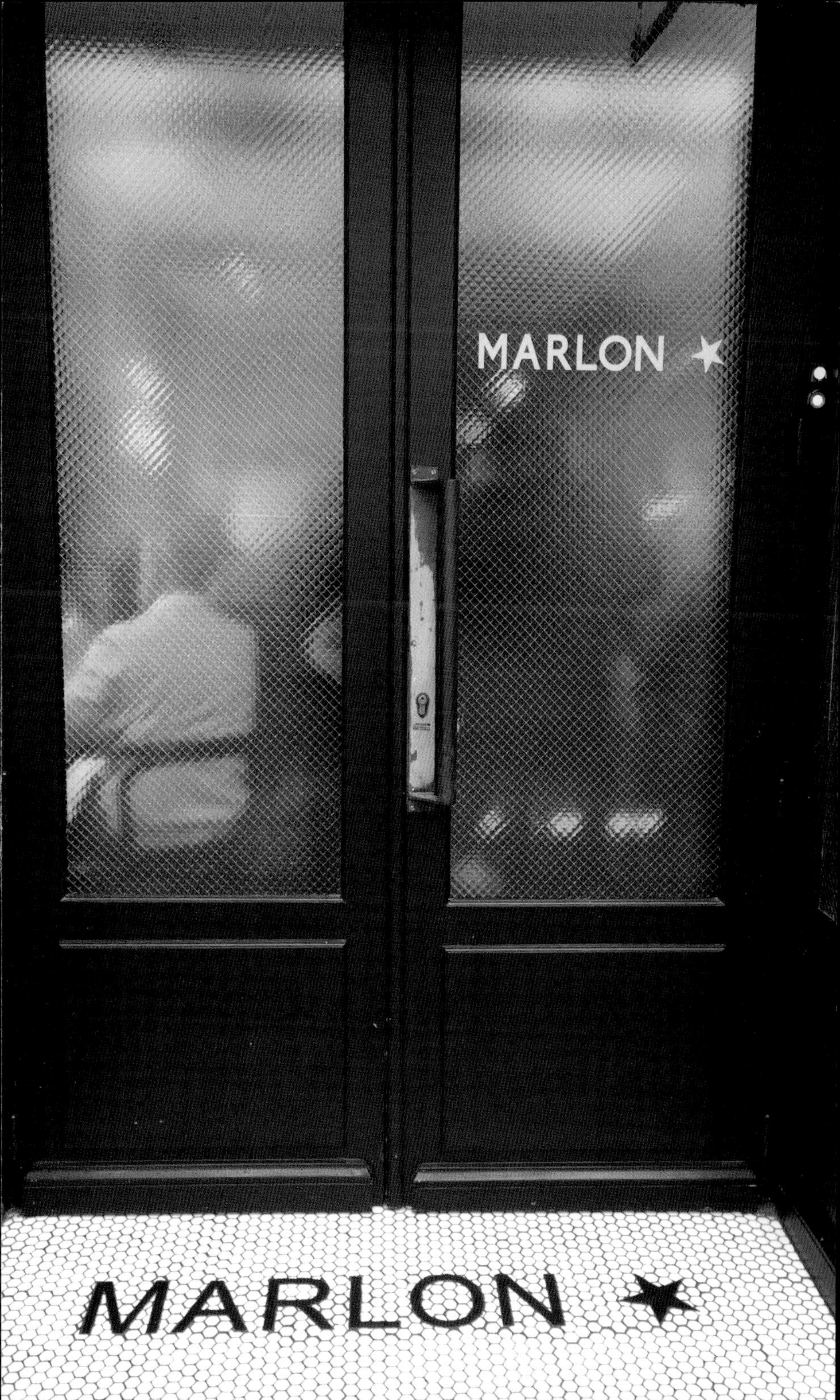
MARLON ★
MARLON ★

A Walk Down Rue Cler

135 Rue Cler is a charming pedestrian-only street lined with a bunch of little stores between rue de Grenelle and Avenue de la Motte-Picquet. There's everything you could want: a bakery, butcher shop, chocolate shop, florist, cheese store, brasserie and several small cafés. **Davoli** [No. 34] is an excellent Italian caterer that set up shop on this street in 1962. Their products are also available at the large Bon Marché grocery store. Across the way, **Famille Mary** [No. 35] is known for their exceptional honey, while **Jeusselin** [No. 37] is a great butcher shop renowned for excellent foie gras. Although the establishment itself is very touristy, I love **Petit Cler**'s facade [No. 29] and authentic Parisian bistro decor. **L'Éclair** [No. 32] will win you over with their upholstered booths, quiet terrace, elegant and eclectic antiques, secondhand objects and a wine list separated into "low cost," "eco," and "business" sections; there's something for every budget. **Maison de Chantilly** [No. 47] is a paradise full of treats, all made with the namesake, immaculate white cream. To do things Parisian-style, take a seat on **Tribeca**'s terrace [No. 36] that gets packed for breakfast. Dishes are varied (pizza, salads, salmon fillet, club sandwiches) and prices are affordable. Once the weather warms, rue Cler smells of flowers and fresh products. During the holidays, there's magic in the air as the street gets covered in Christmas decorations.

Thoumieux's World

136

This place is a hotel, restaurant, brasserie, café and pastry shop all in one, and a 7th Arrondissement must. On the brasserie side, try the Landes duck foie gras, soft-boiled egg with caviar, finely chopped beef tartare and fabulous desserts, including a Tatin tart with thick Bordier cream. India Mahdavi designed the rooms at **Hôtel Thoumieux** [79 rue Saint-Dominique, 7th].

L'Ami Jean

137

Stéphane Jégo is a celebrity chef in Paris and pioneer of French bistronomy. His colorful personality is sure to charm you, as you'll hear him shouting in the kitchen. Waiters answer with "Oui, chef!" It's a real show and one of a kind culinary experience in Paris. Tables at **L'Ami Jean** fill up at lightning speed and people come from far to taste his Southwest French cuisine and delicious rice pudding—a cult dish served with caramel butter and nougatine [27 rue Malar, 7th].

Happiness on the Banks

138

In the summertime, the banks of the Seine transform into a vacation destination with an idle beach vibe. I love the aquatic version of **Rosa Bonheur** [Port des Invalides, 7th] (this spot's first, very festive location is in Parc des Buttes-Chaumont). Float to the rhythm of the Seine's waves and enjoy the magical view of Grand Palais, Pont Alexandre III and the Eiffel Tower. While on the barge, eat tapas, charcuterie, terrine or pizza from the wood-fired oven. This place gets packed at nightfall and is a sure bet for a pleasant evening buzzed by a rosé wine.

A Golden Dome

139 Place des Invalides is impressive with its gilded dome and lawns that lead to Pont Alexandre III. As soon as the weather is suitable, Parisians head here for picnics, to play soccer or hang out on nice park benches. Gaze upon **Chapelle Royale**—also called Église du Dôme— where there's a crypt with Napoleon I's tomb. You can also visit Musée de l'Armée where you'll find Louis the XIV's beautiful armor. Fun fact: The dome was Paris' highest monument until the Eiffel Tower was built. It was re-gilded in 1989, a task that required 12 kilograms (26 ½ pounds) of gold [129 rue de Grenelle, 7th].

The Élysée Cheese Shop

140

Barthélémy
[51 rue de Grenelle, 7th] is a small cheese shop with retro decor that's frozen in time. Nicole Barthélémy has been at the helm here for over 40 years, and it's where Élysée locals have bought their cheese since 1973. Along with creamy Reblochon, soft Brie and runny Saint-Marcellin, their specialty is cow's milk Fontainebleau cheese and Mont d'Or or "Vacherin du Haut-Doubs." Prices are quite high, but you might run into Charlotte Gainsbourg or Catherine Deneuve, who are both regulars.

The Best Chinese Massage

141

Lanqi's great great-uncle went from village to village to soothe peasants with his massages and plants. His worthy descendent now gives the best Chinese massages in Paris at both of her locations with a "Beijing parlor" vibe. There's no fuss or flashy luxury at **Lanqi-Spa**; the rooms are even separated by curtains. Their list of treatments is different and varied with options like suction cups, abdomen massages and reflexology. Try the Tui Na that balances your yin and yang (mind and body). You'll get great results for small prices [48 avenue de Saxe, 7th; 91 rue de Javel, 15th].

A Walk at Champ-de-Mars

142

For a gorgeous view of the Eiffel Tower, head to **Champ-de-Mars** where Parisian go to run and work out. With an area of 24.5 hectares (60 ½ acres), it's one of Paris' biggest gardens. Kick back and take in the view of the Iron Lady [2 Allée Adrienne-Lecouvreur, 7th]—the name Parisians like to give to the Eiffel Tower.

144

The Perfect Dinner Service

143

Since Parisians love to eat, it's no surprise that they're also crazy about everything that has to do with tableware and dishware. Named by American *Vogue* and *Architectural Digest* as one of the best destinations for those who love to host, **Au Bain Marie** [56 rue de l'Université, 7th] has gorgeous old collections, 19th-century silverware and rare utensils you might not have known existed. Leave with a "Rousseau" plate marked with little drawings (owl, lobster or quail) that were inspired by glassmaker Eugène Rousseau's Hokusai Manga collection unveiled in Paris during the 1867 Universal Exposition.

Bir-Hakeim Bridge

144

Pont de Bir-Hakeim provides one of the best views of the Eiffel Tower. With its stone vaults, steel arches and art deco lights, it's a monument in and of itself. Many movie scenes have been filmed here, including one from Inception, starring Leonardo DiCaprio. Take the bridge by boarding Metro line 6 that crosses the Seine between the Passy and Bir-Hakeim stations. You'll catch a breathtaking view at any time of day for the low price of a Metro ticket! Better yet, there's a bicycle and pedestrian path that connects both banks beneath the bridge [quai de Grenelle, 15th].

Beaugrenelle

145

Not a single Parisian would come here if it weren't for the new, most modern shopping mall in Paris. Far from Parisian standards, **Beaugrenelle**'s design has lovely curved, glass facades that create an American atmosphere. A futuristic passageway connects the two oval-shaped sections. Inside, marvel at the sublime glass roof by artist Xavier Veilhan; its colors change depending on the outdoor light. You'll find big fashion brands, a movie theater and a few restaurants. Eat at **Cojean** [12 rue de Linois, 15th], where they make delicious salads and healthy dishes that can be enjoyed on the premises or taken to go.

The Scent Garden

146

Parc Georges-Brassens [Rue des Morillons, 15th] gets its name from the famous singer, who lived at nearby 42 rue Santos-Dumont. It's a great spot to combine many activities if you have kids. You'll find swings, rides, a climbing wall, and you can also go for a pony ride. It's a park with rich natural biodiversity where they organize workshops about grapevines as well as honey, since they have a few beehives. To sharpen your senses, walk through the scent garden filled with aromatic and medicinal plants. The braille labels allow blind people to learn about botany, now why wouldn't you?

146

Great Korean Barbecue

147 Korean hotpot consists of cooking meat directly on a barbecue built into the center of the table. **Bong** [42 rue Blomet, 15th] is one of the best spots in Paris to get the complete experience. They'll serve you a wide variety of small dishes and exquisite marinated meat that you then grill on your individual barbecue. A small tip: Ask for a few lessons on how to eat like Koreans or keep an eye on your neighbors. The atmosphere is laid-back, but know that your clothes and hair will smell of barbecue when you leave!

The Futuristic Park

148 To the great delight of visitors, **Parc André-Citroën** [2 rue Cauchy, 15th] is steeped in a futuristic, visionary spirit on the design front, as well as in it's presented themes. Inaugurated in 1992, it's located at what was the site of the old Citroën car factory. The space—that's open onto the Seine—is equipped for young children, as well as teenagers. You'll find a small square surrounded by 64 water jets, without forgetting the gigantic helium balloon you can go up in—all the way to 150 meters (492 feet) off the ground—to take in the site.

À LA PARISIENNE

French touch

What is meant by a "French touch"? Beautiful materials and craftsmanship. Elegance at every age. The importance of a signature scent, brand awareness, the art of conversation (and the quick retort), and an absolute respect for style and *savoir faire*.

THE CHIC NEIGHBORHOODS

Admire some of the most beautiful Haussmann buildings, marvel at the Grand Palais, discover the hidden treasures of avenue Montaigne, go shopping in the village atmosphere of rue de la Pompe, amble through Place Victor Hugo, visit an exhibition at Palais de Tokyo, and find a shady spot to settle in at Palais de Chaillot...because all roads lead to the Trocadéro.

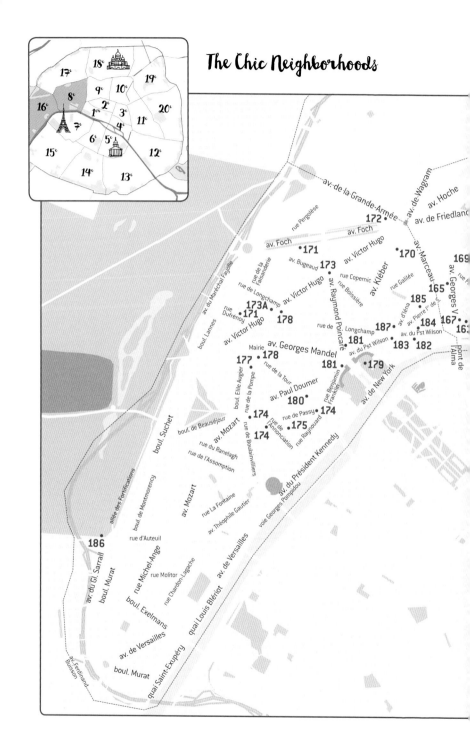

The Chic Neighborhoods

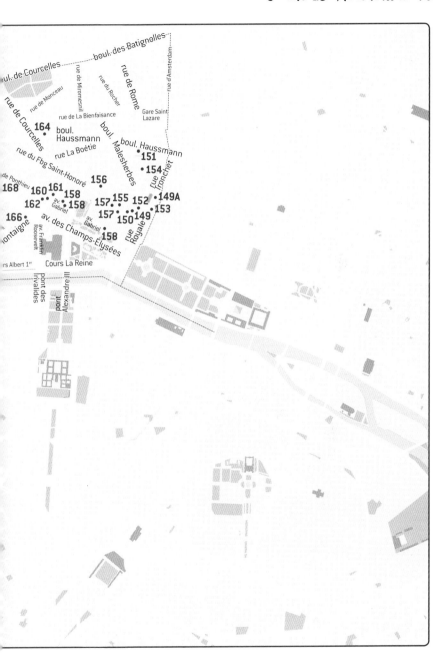

boul. des Batignolles

boul. de Courcelles

rue de Courcelles

rue de Monceau

rue de Miromesnil

rue du Rocher

rue de Rome

rue d'Amsterdam

rue de La Bienfaisance

Gare Saint Lazare

164 boul. Haussmann

rue du Fbg Saint-Honoré

rue La Boétie

boul. Malesherbes

boul. Haussmann

151

154

rue Tronchet

156

de Ponthieu

168 **160** **161** **158**

162 av. Gabriel **158**

157 **155** **152** **149A**

157 **150** **149** **153**

166 av. Gabriel

ntaigne

av. des Champs-Elysées

158

av. Franklin Roosevelt

rue Royale

Cours La Reine

rs Albert 1er

pont des Invalides

pont Alexandre III

D·O·M·SVB·INVOC·S·M·MAGDALENAE

The Madeleine's Secrets

149 I never tire seeing **Église de la Madeleine**, center stage at the end of rue Royale. Look up: Admire its sculptures and staircases adorned with flowers. Pray inside: It's one of the most beautiful churches in the world! The square surrounding it is a must. There are lovely restaurants located all around, including **Paris-London** (A) [No. 16] that I like for its lively atmosphere and terrace with a view of Place de la Madeleine. Continue on your stroll to the small **Marché aux Fleurs** that's been around since 1842. **Place de la Madeleine** was once a huge flower market, and the few remaining businesses are a testament to that heritage. By the eastern entrance (to the right when facing the church) is **Foyer de la Madeleine**, a nonprofit restaurant where the food is made lovingly by the church's nuns. It's almost private and only true Parisians know about it. Nearby is the **Galerie de la Madeleine** passageway [9 Place de la Madeleine, 8th], which connects the square to rue Boissy d'Anglas. To keep the flower theme going, eat at **Bread & Roses** [25 rue Boissy d'Anglas, 8th], an excellent restaurant counter (on the spot or takeout) where you can taste delicious pastries, homemade quiches or healthy organic salads.

149A

Jean-Claude Ellena
In the Hermès secret garden

→》 ·°· 《←

150 Up above one of the most beautiful streets in the world, rue du Faubourg Saint-Honoré, is the most secluded green space in all of Paris. The rooftop garden of **Maison Hermès** [24 rue du Faubourg Saint-Honoré, 8th] is a closely guarded secret. Even fans of the famed Birkin and Kelly bags are unaware of this shimmering green jewel, straight out of a fairy tale, and unfortunately inaccessible to the public. It is home to Jean-Claude Ellena, the house "nose" at the prestigious Maison Hermès since 2004, and among the most gifted perfumers of our time. He created the classics First Van Cleef & Arpels, Déclaration by Cartier, Eau Parfumée au Thé Vert Bulgari, Eau de Campagne Sisley, and Cologne Bigarade for the Éditions de Parfums Frédéric Malle, to name a few. It was in this magical rooftop garden that I had the extraordinary privilege of meeting with him to discuss his fragrance creations.

With a mischievous smile, and a hint of mad genius, he explains his creation process: "I write my fragrance compositions on sheets of paper as you would a musical composition. I start at 8:30 in the morning by reading the compositions from the day before. Then I start writing again. I can write 10 to 15 times a day. I am very disciplined. Sometimes it goes quickly, other times more slowly. Quickly means about 100 tests; slowly is more like 300. The perfume that I composed the most quickly was Un Jardin en Méditerranée, which took three days. I had a very clear idea of what I wanted," said the master perfumer, to whom we owe the legendary perfumes Kelly Calèche, Eau des Merveilles, Un Jardin sur le Nil, and the unforgettable Terre d'Hermès.

His relationship with scents? "For me, they are the building blocks. I know them well. I know their character, their physical properties, their effects and their possible combinations. That's how I handle scents. For me, sandalwood is a sensual wood that is subtle and supple. Cedar is an upright wood. I see their physicality, I touch them. Then they must be presented, structured. It's a relationship that is at once emotional, faithful and unfaithful." Un Jardin sur le Toit, which was created as homage to the garden at 24 rue du Faubourg Saint-Honoré, is a perfume bursting with white florals and apple, a mist of wild grasses and magnolia...

As you amble down rue du Faubourg Saint-Honoré, when you reach the corner of Boissy d'Anglas, look toward the sky. See the little figure on horseback? What you see from the street is what I see up close in the garden—a statue of a soldier on horseback, honoring the origins of Maison Hermès.

DNA in Upper-Crust Paris

Parisian chic is in the DNA of a handful of progeny of well-to-do families who learned to pronounce "Dior," "Chanel" and "Hermès" as early as "mom" and "dad." The Parisian upper middle class has inherited a natural elegance and timeless style that is both highly prescribed and seemingly effortless—but not attainable for the outsider. The members of this elite group from the 16th and 8th Arrondissements attended the same schools and have known each other since before they were born. They are an insular circle of distinguished names—and they can trace each other's lineage back to Napoleon, and spot one another in a crowd: the right it-bag, the right shoes, the right address, the right attitude and, above all, the right friends.

Square Louis XVI

151 Here's another secret spot for architecture and history lovers. At the center of this square stands the expiatory chapel with an original neo-classical, dome-shaped design. It is virtually unknown even though it's where King Louis XVI and Marie-Antoinette were buried. This place of worship is devoted to royal memory and has a wonderful garden surrounded by white rosebushes, as well as stand-in gravestones dedicated to the memory of the French Revolution. Take a moment for the 3,000 victims who were buried here. This was also once the Madeleine's old cemetery [Square Louis XVI, 8th].

Village Royal

152 This small, charming passageway [25 rue Royale, 8th], located steps away from Place de la Madeleine, at the intersection of rue Royale, was once the d'Aguesseau Market with small businesses, butcher shops, cheese shops and fish stores. Nowadays, just a few feet away from thoroughfares, you can dive into a welcoming small-town atmosphere that, being home to Chanel and Dior, has been completely redesigned according to luxury standards. Legend has it that this was the location of the famous 17th-century musketeer barracks of Louis XIII's royal guards. In the summertime, eat on the quiet terrace at **Le Village** [1 Cité Berryer, 8th], which is part of the renowned hoteliers and restaurateurs Costes brothers' empire.

The Mustard Bar

153

Mustard is a part of French expertise; you'll find jars of it everywhere! Everyone knows about Dijon mustard, but do you know the origins of Maison Maille? As the story goes, distiller and vinegar maker Antoine-Claude Maille created an antiseptic, vinegar-based concoction to save Marseille's residents from the plague. In 1747, his son—also named Antoine-Claude—opened his first shop in Paris and became the official supplier for the court of King Louis XV. In 1845, Antoine-Claude junior's son Robert opened the first Maille boutique in Dijon, the star mustard producing area in Burgundy. This is how Dijon mustard became famous. To discover all the subtleties of mustard, visit the one-of-a-kind **Boutique Maille** [6 Place de la Madeleine, 8th], which opened in honor of the brand's 250th anniversary. They have a mustard bar where you can refill your jars with mustard fresh from the pump. Discover more daring flavors: mustard with blue cheese, Chablis and black truffle or lemon and harissa. Talk to the experts to find the best mustard and food pairings depending on desired intensity: mild, medium or hot.

"Add three letters, and Paris becomes Paradise."

Jules Renard

Hidden Zo

156

This is MY canteen, since I lived nearby at Place Beauvau for five years. Located steps away from the Palais de l'Élysée on a small hidden street, **Zo** [13 rue Montalivet, 8th] has kept up the food quality and international vibe through the years. I like the varied menu that isn't restricted to a single style of cuisine, which is rather rare in Paris. You can eat good sushi, since there's a sushi chef on the premises, or order a tartare, a burger, absolutely delicious pasta or a beet carpaccio. There's something for everyone in a pretention-free atmosphere. In the summertime, the restaurant also has a lovely terrace in the **Pavillon des Lettres** courtyard [12 rue des Saussaies, 8th]. This is a nice, intimate, centrally located hotel that's definitely a sure bet, since it's right by the Élysée.

Hôtel Bedford

154

This grandiose hotel is very well located and reasonably priced. Rooms are comfortable and the setting is classically Parisian. Even when I'm not staying at the hotel, I like to go for brunch at the hotel's Restaurant **Le Victoria** [17 rue de l'Arcade, 8th]. Its gorgeous colored glass roof provides the perfect lighting for marveling at the frescoes, angels and walls decorated with sumptuous etchings. It's truly magnificent.

Buddha Hotel

155

Right by the Faubourg Saint-Honoré and the Élysée, you'll find the brand-new **Buddha-Bar Hotel** [4 rue d'Anjou, 8th] with its sublime 200-square-meter (2,150-square-foot) paved terrace. Located in a majestic 18th-century building, the hotel organizes festive happy hours with DJs every Thursday, allowing you to watch the chic Parisian crowd and have a drink beneath white lanterns that light up when the sun goes down. This part of the 8th arrondissement isn't necessarily the liveliest when it comes to hip parties, but it's by far one of Paris' chicest and most magical quarters.

The Lancôme Cocoons

157

This is where the famous French brand **Lancôme** [29 rue du Faubourg Saint-Honoré, 8th] dispenses its knowledge. The ground floor is a boutique and makeup space, while the 1st floor is devoted to treatments. I love the treatment cabins' cocoon feel on the upper floor. It's like being transported into a futuristic setting where you forget the present, the locale and space for the duration of a unique facial. Try a body massage with Thibault, who is very well known by the house's regular clients—as well as its VIPs. He combines massage therapy and energetic techniques to magically rebalance your chakras. Right across the street, you'll find the **Salon Coiff1rst** [52 rue du Faubourg Saint-Honoré, 8th], established at the back of a courtyard beneath a huge skylight that allows hairdressers and colorists to work in the sunlight.

Gabriel Avenue

158

From Place de la Concorde, take gorgeous Avenue Gabriel, lined with hundred-year-old trees that border many embassies. It's an oasis of greenery right in the heart of the city. Pass by **Espace Pierre Cardin** [No. 1] that houses a theater and beautiful reception hall. Continue on your way and walk along the Palais de l'Élysée's gardens. You'll see the *Grille du Coq* (gate with an ornate rooster), at the impressive entrance to the French president's home. The gate was installed in 1905. After crossing avenue de Marigny, look for the huge red door on your right. It's **La Réserve** [No. 42], a new ultra luxurious five-star hotel. Their suites are some of the most expensive in Paris and come with a view of the Eiffel Tower and the Grand Palais. I love having coffee there or heading to the bar for a business meeting. Right across the street is **Laurent** Restaurant [No. 41], an institution of Parisian gastronomy. The food is incredibly good, the service impeccable and the decor super-classic. It's a traditional place where French expertise takes center stage. The bay windows look out onto the lovely Carré Marigny garden. When the weather is suitable, tables are set on the garden terrace from noon to night. [avenue Gabriel, 8th].

The Most Beautiful Walk in the World

159 My favorite stroll to take in Paris starts at Place Beauvau, right by the Élysée, from where I walk to the Invalides. Take Avenue de Marigny, a sublime tree-lined thoroughfare that takes you by Jardins de l'Élysée. Pass by Théâtre Marigny and cross Avenue des Champs-Élysées. Let yourself be awestruck by the Grand Palais and Petit Palais, both grandiose at any hour of the day. Then, cross my favorite bridge, the Pont Alexandre III. You'll probably see newlywed couples in the middle of a photo shoot. Inaugurated for the 1900 Universal Exposition, this bridge is impressive with its gorgeous street lamps and view of the Eiffel Tower. In front of you, Les Invalides' golden dome is an incredible sight. You've seen the two most beautiful Parisian monuments in the span of 10 minutes. Is your heart pounding? Mine, too.

169

The New Kinugawa

162 **Kinugawa** is a Japanese gastronomy institution in Paris [9 rue du Mont Thabor, 1st]. They just opened another location on rue Jean Mermoz [1 bis rue Jean Mermoz, 8th] in an old restaurant well known to Parisians. The new location is an excellent spot to enjoy exquisite sashimi and the must-try grilled black cod marinated in miso sauce. It's actually considered one of the 25 best dishes in Paris. Try the Maguro No Taruto appetizer, made with minced tuna on a crispy galette, white truffle tarama and yuzukosho sauce. That says it all.

A Beloved Boudoir

160 Behind the black door is a refuge for those in the know—the hidden, intimate atmosphere of **Mathis** [3 rue de Ponthieu, 8th]: a cocktail bar open all night long. Those who like to party know the way. I love the boudoir decor with red velvet booths and chandeliers. This cult destination was once very private and patronized by Yves Saint Laurent and his glamorous guests. The bar and restaurant section was recently taken over by the guys at Experimental Group (see page 183). It's a timeless icon of Parisian nightlife that avoids passing trends.

The Perfect Business Restaurant

161 It's impossible not to mention **Market** [15 Avenue Matignon, 8th], my favorite spot for a business lunch. Tables are spaced out, far from the Parisian norm. You'll see lots of men in suits and ties. I've actually crossed paths with Lenny Kravitz and Woody Allen there. The menu is Asian-inspired and they serve an excellent tuna tartare. Once the weather warms, head out onto the pretty terrace from where you can see the Eiffel Tower. It's rather quiet in the evening when the clientele is more touristy and international. You're right by the Champs-Élysées, the Grand Palais and the Petit Palais. All is good.

Upper Montaigne

163

High up on the very chic avenue Montaigne, on the roof of **Théâtre des Champs-Élysées**, you'll find **Maison Blanche** (A) [15 avenue Montaigne, 8th], one of the nicest restaurants in the City of Light. It has a breathtaking view of the Eiffel Tower, the Seine and Les Invalides' dome. In the summer, the relaxed, almost aerial terrace is a sought-after gem for the business crowd. In the evening, it's a very romantic spot that's often the setting for marriage proposals, family parties and privileged events worth celebrating. It's a must for special occasions or just to take advantage of the beautiful setting. While you're there, head over to **Manko** right next door [No. 15 as well]: a new spot that serves Peruvian cuisine in a cabaret-bar.

The Museum Café

164

The **Musée Jaquemart-André** [158 boulevard Haussmann, 8th] is located in a splendid mansion hotel. It is home to one of the most beautiful private art collections in Paris, containing pieces from the Italian Renaissance to 18th-century France. Works by Rembrandt, Botticelli and Bellini are part of the permanent collection, and the space also hosts many temporary exhibits. I love the castle-museum atmosphere, stately lounges, monumental staircase, winter garden and private apartments. Take a seat in the courtyard and feel the energy of this unique place that once belonged to two art lovers: Nélie Jaquemart and Édouard André. **Café Jaquemart-André**—the ultimate snobbery for lovers of art and private spaces—is located inside the museum, and admission is free. It's one of the prettiest tearooms in all of Paris, but shh, it's a secret.

Jeff Leatham's Flowers

165

Gwyneth Paltrow, Kate Moss and George Clooney: All the stars call on him for their parties or special events. For those who aren't lucky enough to stay at **George V** [31 Avenue George V, 8th], it's worth the detour if only to see the impressive floral creations by famed floral artistic director, Jeff Leatham. The ex-model—who learned the tricks of the trade from his florist father—is a trendy star in the luxury hotel flower arrangement world. Take the opportunity to have a drink at the bar as you listen to the talented pianist. Gaze at the splendor around you, in one of the most beautiful hotels in the world.

The Triangle d'Or's Concept Store

166

Style and fashion lovers: **Montaigne Market** [57 Avenue Montaigne, 8th] is a must-see for high fashion and designers in the heart of Paris' Triangle d'Or—a perimeter delineated by Champs-Élysées, avenue George V and avenue Montaigne), where you'll find accessories, shoes, designer clothing, etc. This luxury concept store that brings together the greatest brands under one roof is the perfect spot to find the right silhouette, straight from the catwalk...before searching for equivalents in box stores.

165

The Crazy Horse's Dancers

167 Moulin Rouge, Crazy Horse or Lido: If you can only see one of them, I recommend **Crazy Horse** [12 Avenue George V, 8ᵗʰ], hands down. It's Paris' most glamorous, iconic cabaret bar where big names collaborate, such as Christian Louboutin, who was the first designer invited to create four scenes for them in 2012. Dita Von Teese, Noémie Lenoir and Arielle Dombasle have also taken the stage there. It's voluptuous, sensual and creative. Come enjoy a colorful, artistic and one hundred percent burlesque show in an intimate, red and very Parisian setting. You can eat on the premises or take a seat for the show. A good plan would be to watch the show from the bar at the back since it's less expensive and more captivating.

Guerlain Institute

168 **Boutique Guerlain** [68 Avenue des Champs-Élysées, 8ᵗʰ], at the Champps-Élysées, is the perfect spot to connect with the psirit of the great beauty-and-perfume house. The boutique was entirely renovated by architect Peter Marino in 2013. In the historic part, smell exclusive creations by L'Art et la Matière and Les Parisiennes. Learn about the legendary brand's history, and check out impressive collection of bee-marked vials inspired by Empress Eugénie, wife of Napoléon III. In the basement, the chic restaurant **Le 68** serves a menu created by chef Guy Martin. The Institut is on the 2ⁿᵈ floor, in the Guerlain family's old apartments. In a sumptuous orchid-filled lounge, discover the "slippers ritual" (removing your shoes and donning very pretty slippers), enjoy a cup of tea and get a private consultation to determine how your personalized care will go.

The Anastasia Plate

169 Parisians rarely meet on the Champs-Élysées. They actually avoid the avenue as much as possible! If you're in the area, **Café Kousmichoff** [71 avenue des Champs-Élysées, 8th], located above the **Kusmi** boutique, serves Franco-Russian cuisine and its famous Kusmi teas. Order the "Tsar" salad (chicken Caesar), salmon gravlax or Anastasia plate (smoked salmon, king crab, salmon roe, tarama, cucumbers, baby lettuce, blinis and fresh cream) or the Bien-être plate (salmon tartare, vegetable skewers, soup of the day, quinoa tabbouleh and mesclun). The setting is gorgeous and quiet, and you'll forget about the Champs' tumult for a bit.

A Rooftop Champagne Bar

170 There are very few rooftop terraces in Paris where you can drink a glass of champagne while keeping an eye on the Eiffel Tower. The terrace on the **Hôtel Raphael**'s [17 avenue Kléber, 16th] 7th floor rooftop is, in my opinion, the most romantic place on Earth. Tables are spread out in a little garden full of rosebushes meant to preserve the privacy of the exclusive clientele. Arrive early for happy hour, especially on nice, sunny days. Enjoy a delectable glass of champagne with a few mini pastries for a special occasion. It's pricey, but the view is priceless. You can also eat in their restaurant, with its draped fabrics and stylish upholstery.

173

Fortune Magnet

171 Avenue Foch is one of 12 avenues that start at Place de l'Étoile and one of the most prestigious. It's the widest avenue in Paris, the most prominent destination that attracts the greatest fortunes in the world. Its layout is unique with green spaces and 10 meters (33 feet) of private garden on either side at every address. To venture into these historic buildings, go for a free visit at the **Musée d'Ennery** [No. 59], a gorgeous, completely restored mansion hotel filled with treasure that dates back to the 19th century. Visits are only allowed with a reservation and are conducted in small, guided groups. At the very end of avenue Foch is the Porte Dauphine and the beginning of Bois de Boulogne. For a yummy stop, take rue de la Faisanderie on your left and head straight to **Schou** [No. 96], my favorite spot in Paris to pick up pastries, croissants, apple turnovers...or whatever makes you salivate.

Lenny Kravitz's Arc

172 The first stone of the Arc de Triomphe was laid in 1836, in the summer heat. Located in a mansion hotel in the monument's shadow, **Victoria 1836** [12 rue de Presbourg, 16th] is a sublime restaurant that was entirely redecorated by Parisian designer Sarah Lavoine. It has an exceptional view of Place de l'Étoile, and it's full of velvet, brass lighting fixtures, mirror tricks and Saint-Laurent marble. Request a spot in the library for a quiet date, or take a seat at the bar for a drink with friends. Downstairs is home to **L'Arc**, the very chic nightclub where Lenny Kravitz is the artistic director.

Place Victor Hugo

173 Avenue Victor Hugo often gets a bad rap for being too stuffy. I actually find it to be the perfect spot for doing a bit of quiet shopping. From the Arc de Triomphe, walk to Place Victor Hugo and wander around **La Ferme d'Hugo** [5 Place Victor Hugo, 16th], a fruit and vegetable concept store. There's a great takeout salad bar and a fine selection of up-and-coming foodie brands inside. For an atmosphere straight out of the roaring twenties and the Belle Époque, eat at **Le Petit Rétro** [5 rue Mesnil, 16th]. Established in 1904, it's one of the last *real* Parisian bistros. In fact, it's registered as a historical monument. Explore the tasty French menu in a setting decorated with wrought iron lighting fixtures and original moldings. After dining, have coffee at **You Decide** (A) [152 avenue Victor Hugo, 16th], a little hidden gem where you can drink herbal tea and excellent coffee or eat eggs Benedict, homemade brioche and avocado. Prices are low and food is made with organic ingredients.

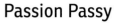

Passion Passy

174 The women in this chic neighborhood go to rue de Passy to wander around and spend time with their girlfriends. You'll find well-known brand names like Zara, Guerlain and Kiehl's alongside a few businesses that are frozen in time, like **Passy Plaza**. At the very end of the des Carrières cul-de-sac is **Villa Passy** [No. 4], a small café with a lovely summertime terrace. Stop in at **La Maison Desgranges** bakery [6 rue de Passy, 16ᵗʰ] for a few culinary delights before going to the **Marché Couvert de Passy** [1 rue Bois le Vent, 16ᵗʰ], located in a covered market with a 1950s style that contrasts sharply with 16ᵗʰ-Arrondissement Haussmannian architecture. There are 20 or so stands: fishmonger, cheese shop, florist, etc. You might cross paths with chef Alain Ducasse. It's a good opportunity to combine getting the essentials for a home-cooked meal with "window" shopping.

A Very Cool Tearoom

175 At the very end of rue Jean Boulogne, there's a quiet, hidden little square that even some of the locals don't know about. There, you'll find a spot full of regulars that's been open for over 30 years: **Thé Cool** [10 rue Jean Bologne, 16ᵗʰ]. Sarah Lavoine redecorated the very hip space with a luminous, cozy 1950s retro style, including vintage posters from *Lui* magazine hanging on the walls. Order the very healthy quinoa salad, a fresh juice that plays the retro card and a huge piece of lemon pie for dessert.

La Pompe's Village Feel

176

At the intersection of rue de la Tour and rue de la Pompe, you'll be thrown into a village setting. The small church, Swiss chalet, bakery, fish shop and butcher shop sit side by side in an atmosphere full of know-how and refined products. I love running errands there. I can grab a farmer's chicken at **Boucherie de la Tour** [64 rue de la Pompe, 16th] and cheese from an incredible selection at **Aux Bons Fromages** [No. 64 as well]. Take owner Claude's sage advice and choose the perfect bleu d'Auvergne, Reblochon or creamy goat cheese. Claude's mother, Colette, is at the cash. For fresh vegetables, just head across the street. Enjoy!

Knitters' Den

177

Here's an awesome shop concept where they specialize in wool and knitwear, along with teaching the art of knitting. There are a few shops like this around Paris, and **Une Maille à l'Endroit** [45 rue de la Pompe, 16th] is the newbie. You'll find an wide selection of yarn (wool, alpaca, cashmere, bamboo, linen) nicely organized in an impressive wall storage unit, along with knitting books, needles and knitting machines. It's like a candy store for stitch lovers.

Pilates and Pastries

178 I go to **Studio Pilates 16** [111 rue de Longchamp, 16th] to take yoga and Pilates classes in small groups. I love the size of the crowd and highly qualified teachers. Choose Paola for some vinyasa yoga or Sandrine Bridoux, who subscribes to American Tara Stiles' strala yoga. On your way out, treat yourself to a little something at **Pâtisserie des Rêves**, one of the best pastry shops in Paris that happens to be in the same building. They have a unique choux pastry bar and a charming tearoom.

Comme des Poissons

180 With just nine seats, this place is tiny. It's a bit cramped, but oh so charming! The Japanese eatery doesn't look like much, but locals are crazy about it, and its authentic character is a nice change of pace. Have a seat on one of the stools at **Comme des Poissons'** [24 rue de la Tour, 16th] long counter. Enjoy the chef's creations concocted for the joy of your taste buds. Exquisite maki and sashimi are served in a big rice bowl in a convivial setting with good atmosphere. You'll need a reservation.

The Trocadéro Gardens

179 Right by the impressive **Palais de Chaillot** is the **Jardins du Trocadéro**, which was created for the 1878 Universal Exposition. To get there, take the Place du Trocadéro steps or go around the Palais de Chaillot on the far left. Grab a bench and enjoy some tranquility in the shadow of the Eiffel Tower. It's a charming spot with small ponds, a pretty bridge and sculptures. Perfect for strolling, reading, kissing... Take in the energy of ancestral trees; breathe in the spirit of Paris. Then, walk below Palais de Chaillot and sit down by the **Fontaine de Varsovie**, facing the impressive water cannons [Place du Trocadéro and du 11 Novembre, 16th].

By the Eiffel Tower

181

The Trocadéro is the first place I go after arriving in Paris to anchor myself into the city's energy. To discuss the changing world on a terrace shaded by your sunglasses, head to **Carette** [4 Place du Trocadéro, 16th]. Yes, it's very touristy, but it remains a gathering spot for real Parisians in the 16th Arrondissement and the best place to meet up. Eat an apple turnover or from a delicious assortment of sweets on the spot. Later on, enjoy happy hour or dinner at **Café de l'Homme** [17 Place du Trocadéro, 16th], an exceptional eatery located inside the Musée de l'Homme. During the summer, they have a great terrace in town with a view of the Eiffel Tower.

Bleu, Tokyo and Yoyo

182

Those who love a trendy, artsy vibe should make sure to check out **Palais de Tokyo** [13 avenue du Président Wilson, 16th], which is considered to be a contemporary art rebel. Take in an exhibit and read in the bookstore that's open until midnight. Grab a bite to eat at the central café or, for a breathtaking view of the Eiffel Tower in a hip, refined atmosphere, go to the first floor of **Monsieur Bleu** [20 avenue de New York, 16th]. During the summer, the terrace is *the* place to be. To prolong the fun until the very end of the night, head to **Yoyo**, the Palais de Tokyo's nightclub and one of the best destinations in town for seasoned night owls.

The Same View as Gustave Eiffel

183

One of Paris' most prestigious spots is at the **Shangri-La Hotel** [10 avenue d'Iéna, 16th]. On the hotel's 7th floor, the Suite Shangri-La is 220 square meters (2,350 square feet) in size, with a 100-square-meter (1,075-square-foot) private terrace. The panoramic view spans from Montmartre to Trocadéro, passing by the Grand-Palais, Notre-Dame de Paris, Pont Alexandre III, the Panthéon, Les Invalides, Quai Branly and the Eiffel Tower. The suite costs €20,000 a night. Fun fact: The house next door belonged to Gustave Eiffel [5 Place d'Iéna, 16th].

The Fashion Museum

184

I love **Palais Galliera** [10 avenue Pierre 1er de Serbie, 16th] for its Italian Renaissance style. Built in 1888, it houses the **Musée de la Mode de la Ville de Paris**. Eat at **Galliera** [No. 15], facing a small adjacent square filled with roses, where you can get a view of the palace. After your visit to the museum, check out the garden, which you can enter on avenue du Président Wilson. It has a lovely, quiet pond and magnificent lime trees, chestnut trees and sequoias. The palace was originally designed to house the art collection of philanthropist Duchess de Galliera Marie Brignole-Sale. Her initials are above the entrance gate.

Namaste at the Tigre

185

A few steps away from Place du Trocadéro, you can go into a building's courtyard and walk through a small garden: Here you are in the tiger's den. A unique and quirky wellness concept in the City of Light, the **Tigre Yoga Club** [19 rue de Chaillot, 16th] has a B-space (bar-bistro-boutique-*bibliothèque* [library]) by Café Pinson, a relaxation space with spiritual books, photo exhibits, yoga clothing and massage rooms, including one where they practice Thai massage. This destination, with a second location on the Left Bank, was designed as a labyrinth with many yoga, Pilates and meditation rooms.

Auteuil Greenhouses

186

Are you a botany lover? Do you have children? Here's an out-of-the-ordinary activity that will transport you into a unique tropical atmosphere. Little known to actual Parisians, the **Serres d'Auteuil** [3 avenue de la Porte d'Auteuil, 16th], built in 1761, is home to over 5,500 species of plants and trees from faraway countries. They grow splendidly beneath the huge glass and metal structure. The space is charming and romantic, and you can get a guided tour. You just need to buy a Metro ticket and it is free.

The Buddhist Garden's Giant Bamboos

187

Want to escape? Between shopping sprees, discover Asian art and Japanese culture in the heart of Paris at **Musée Guimet** [6 Place d'Iéna, 16th], a secret shared by only a few Parisians. Learn the art of the tea ceremony in the Chashitsu tea pavilion. Even more secret: **Hôtel d'Heidelbach's Buddhist garden** [19 Avenue d'Iéna, 16th]. It's a gorgeous mansion hotel that's home to the **Panthéon Bouddhique**, which is devoted to Émile Guimet's private collection of religious sculptures. The garden is at the very back of the rooms on the ground floor and has lanterns, ponds, stone walkways, small wooden bridges and giant bamboos. And it's free!

Véronique André
Food critic of the top chefs

188 She reviews an average of 260 restaurants a year, knows all the top-rated chefs and the best restaurants in Paris, and has *haute cuisine* press agents trembling in their boots. Food critic at *Le Figaro*, Véronique André is the most respected writer on the Parisian culinary scene. Her reviews are a feast for the senses, and her colorful personality leaves no one indifferent. She has an opinion on everything, and will tell you LOUD AND CLEAR when she finds something disgusting or, on the other hand, will wholeheartedly endorse what she loves, and offer her unwavering support.

She knows the seasoned ways of Alain Ducasse and the young, emerging sous-chefs, and which bistros serve the best Peking duck, the perfect lemon tart and the top foie gras. She is the only one who could get away with requesting a quirky menu from chef Alain Passard because she's on a diet. She has zero tolerance for bad service, but delights in discovering new gems, provided they are in chic neighborhoods. The major restaurants in Paris call on her impressive expertise to get constructive criticism.

So what are her thoughts on French cuisine today? "It's a bit too full of itself. It still believes it is the best in the world, but young chefs all over the world are learning about French cuisine, while also considering foreign cuisine and tastes with humility and interest." Who is her favorite chef? "It changes, because chefs are always changing, but I adore what Alain Passard is doing. He's extraordinary. He discovered organic 20 years before the rest of the world. He's a master of produce, and his cooking techniques and inventiveness are unparalleled."

In addition to her reviews for major media outlets, she has written several books, including one on the cuisine at the Élysée (residence of the French president) under then President Nicholas Sarkozy—a highly guarded place that she was able to access thanks to her reputation for professionalism and discretion. "While at the Élysée, I discovered the people who work behind the scenes, beyond the politics. Presidents come and go, but these people stay," she said. While in Paris, you might bump into her in a five-star hotel or a new culinary hot spot, enjoying one of her three favorite dishes (chicken with morel mushrooms, caviar and artichoke risotto) with a glass of Saint-Julien.

Her top recommendations for the 8th and 16th Arrondissements? **Apicius**, chef Jean-Pierre Vigato [20 rue d'Artois, 8th]; **Le Grand Restaurant**, chef Jean-François Piège [7 rue d'Aguesseau, 8th]; **Le Bristol**, chef Éric Frechon [112 rue du Faubourg Saint-Honoré, 8th]; **Maison Blanche** [15 avenue Montaigne, 8th]; **L'Orangerie** in the Hôtel George V [31 avenue George V, 8th], chef David Bizet; and the brasserie **Le Flandrin** [4 Place Tattegrain, 16th].

SoPi
and
CANAL SAINT-MARTIN

Discover the hotspots in SoPi (South Pigalle),
give in to temptation in the many gourmet stores
along rue des Martyrs, take in the rich atmosphere
of the faubourg Saint-Martin—a blend of
bourgeois-boho and Indian, and forget about
time as you stroll along the picturesque
Canal Saint-Martin.

SoPi and Canal Saint-Martin

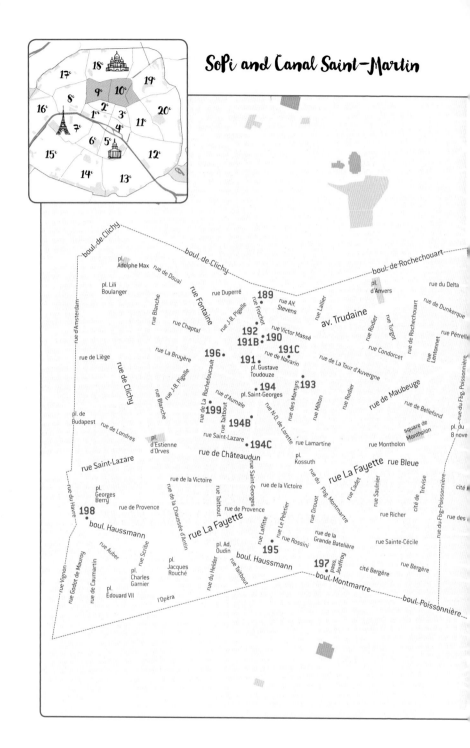

boul. de la Chapelle

boul. de La Villette

rue Louis Blanc

rue Ph. de Girard

rue de Château Landon

rue de l'Aqueduc

rue du Fbg Saint-Martin

rue de Maubeuge

rue du Fbg Saint-Denis

rue de l'Aqueduc

rue La Fayette

boul. de-la-Villette

boul. Magenta

boul. Magenta

pl. de
Roubaix

Gare
du Nord

pl. D.
September

rue Louis Blanc

quai de Jemmapes

boul. Magenta

rue de Dunkerque

rue La Fayette

rue Ph.
de Girard

rue Eugène Varlin

canal Saint-Martin

rue Francis
Jammes

neville

pl. de
Valenciennes

rue d'Alsace

rue du Fbg Saint-Martin

rue Boy Zelenski

pl. du
Colonel
Fabien

pl. Franz
Liszt

rue des Petits Hôtels

quai de Valmy

av. Claude Vellefaux

boul. de-La-Villette

942

rue de Chabrol

pl. du 11 novembre 1918

av. de Verdun

rue de la Grange aux Belles

Juliette Dodu

rue d'Hauteville

rue du 8 mai 1945

rue des Récollets

av. Claude Vellefaux

rue Ste-Marthe

pl. Ste
Marthe

rue de Paradis

• 204

203 •

rue de la Fidélite

rue Bichat

• 211

Écuries

rue Martel

boul. Magenta

rue des Vinaigriers

square des
Récollets

206B

av. Claude Vellefaux

passage Hebard

• 201

rue du Fbg Saint-Denis

boul. de Strasbourg

rue de Nancy

• 200

rue Lucien
Sampaix

206 •

207

210 •
208

canal Saint-Martin

av. Richerand

rue du Buisson

cour des
Petites Écuries

202 •

205

passage

Brady

Mairie

rue du Château d'Eau

pl.
Jacques
Bonsergent

rue de Lancry

rue de Marseille

rue Alibert

rue Bichat

av. Parmentier

rue Saint-Maur

rue d'Enghien

boul. du Faubourg Saint-Martin

rue Beaurepaire

quai de Jemmapes

rue du Fbg du Temple

rue de l'Échiquier

• 209

rue Bouchardon

rue René Boulanger

boul. Magenta

quai de Valmy

boul. Bonne-Nouvelle

boul. Saint-Martin

SoPi

189 If you walk south of Pigalle Metro all the way to Notre-Dame-de-Lorette Metro—within the perimeter formed more or less by rue Blanche, rue de Maubeuge, rue de Rochechouart, avenue Trudains and boulevard de Clichy—you'll notice the famed SoPi signs everywhere. What's SoPi? It's the signature of one of Paris' most exciting neighborhoods. It also stands in for "South Pigalle," much like New York's SoHo (South of Houston Street). The area is artsy, boho and hip with a scandalous past thanks to the emblematic Moulin Rouge. SoPi has its own reinvented identity with a new creative Paris coming out of the woodwork. This change is motivated by a moderately bourgeois golden youth who dreams of breaking free from traditional confines.

The Hipster Florist

190

At age 32, Pierre Banchereau left his head-hunting business job to become a florist. He opened his own shop, **Debeaulieu** [30 rue Henry Monnier, 9th], as homage to his grandparents who passed on their passion for flowers to him. As a SoPi lover, he dreamt of an airy space that reflected his creativity, preferably on rue Henry Monnier for its family vibe and artistic style. Each bouquet is unique at his shop, which is full of vases culled from Paris' best secondhand stores. He's truly a blooming floral designer; Cerruti and Louis Vuitton are among his clients.

The No-Stress Square

191

Place Gustave Toudouze is one of my favorites for a cup of coffee in a quiet spot, away from traffic. There aren't any extraordinary restaurants here, only a rather ordinary Indian eatery. Instead, go for coffee or a happy hour drink on the terrace of **No Stress Café** (A) [No. 2] alongside the neighborhood's boho residents. For a little something to eat, head a bit farther up rue Henry Monnier and try **Buvette** (B) [No. 28], which has a New-York atmosphere. Order their tartine (toast) with Bayonne ham or a few scones with an American-style latte, topped with pretty designs worthy of the greatest baristas. The nearby **Hôtel Amour** (C) [8 rue de Navarin, 9th] has one of the most beautiful private terraces during the summer.

The Experimental Group

⇢⇢ ⸰⸰ ⇠⇠

192

This group manages and owns restaurants, wine and cocktail bars, and hotels in Paris, London, New York and Ibiza. So who exactly are they? The Experimental Group is composed of three friends with very different, though complementary, backgrounds (Romée de Goriainoff, Olivier Bon and Pierre-Charles Cros), who share a passion for living well: eating well, drinking well, entertaining well and traveling well. In Paris, their name is synonymous with the latest trends. They're the masterminds behind **Experimental Cocktail Club**, **Prescription Cocktail Club**, **Ballroom du Beef Club**, **Compagnie des Vins Surnaturels**, Restaurant de l'**Hôtel Bachaumont**, **Grand Pigalle Hôtel** (29 rue Victor Massé, 9th), and **Hôtel Mathis**, to name a few.

What is their trademark? "We create spaces where we would want to be customers. That is our guiding principle. We have always loved good food, good wine and traveling. The project is part of a desire to create places in different countries that offer high quality at every stage of an experience: the produce, the wine, the cocktails, the hotel experience," they explain in unison. So who does what? "We certainly complement each other, and we like to think we do things collectively. All major decisions are made collectively. No one has a specific job title—for example, no one is officially in charge of finance or HR. Our goal has always been to avoid being stuck in an office doing repetitive work."

Big fans of American and London steakhouses, they've been inspired by the New York concept where restaurateurs work directly with farmers, without intermediaries. "We always wanted to open one in Paris, and we began to think about what is required for a steakhouse, starting with the meat supply. Bit by bit, we've examined the food production industry in Europe in order to find the best meat, the best farmers. This led us to Yorkshire where we met Tim Wilson, which allowed us finally to realize our dream of offering farm-to-table meat, with the Beef Club restaurants. No intermediary butchers, but directly from the farmer to the table."

What enthuses Parisians today? "Overall, there is a desire to know the story behind the restaurants where they eat, where the food comes from, and how it is served. People are less concerned with whether a place is trendy or not. We've also been seeing more international cuisine: Korean, Japanese and Mexican cuisine, which have all been branded as "ethnic," are really starting to be taken seriously by Parisians."

Martyrs' Sinful Delights

193

Rue des Martyrs is SoPi's epicenter packed with delicious treats. Do your senses a favor by walking along this street. Taste its delights guilt-free, knowing that walking up the steep hill will help you to burn off some of the calories you take in along the way. Among the must-tries from bottom to top, I'll mention Olivier Baussan's Provençale olive oils at **Première Pression Provence** [No. 9], **La Chambre aux Confitures**'s organic jams [No. 9], **Yoom**'s amazing dim sum [No. 20], **Terra Corsa**'s authentic Corsican products [No. 42], **Popelini**'s cream-of-the-crop choux pastry [No. 44] and **Rose Bakery**'s incredible pastries and Sunday brunches [No. 46]. A bit higher up, I love **Café Marlette**'s [No. 51] cozy vibe, small terrace and famous Marlette brunch, complete with scones, fresh cheese, jambon de Paris (Parisian ham), assorted breads and jams, compote and granola. At the intersection of avenue Trudaine, at the very top of the street, **KB Caféshop** [53 Avenue Trudaine] is a freelancers' headquarters and a place to see and be seen.

Place Saint-Georges

194

This tiny circular square is one of the 9th arrondissement's chicest. The central bust erected in honor of illustrator Paul Gavarni was once a drinking fountain for horses. This place attracts a hip Parisian crowd: As I wrote these lines, fashion mag *ELLE France's* editor-in-chief was in the middle of a photo shoot at À la **Place Saint-Georges** café (A) [No. 60]. If you're looking for a bite to eat in the area, **Le Bon Georges** (B) [45 rue Saint-Georges], south of the square, is a very good bistro with a quintessentially Parisian atmosphere. The excellent **Salsamenteria di Parma** (C) eatery is also just bit lower down on rue Saint-Georges [No. 40].

A Balanced pH Level

195

Lovers of raw food, fresh ingredients and vegan restaurants will want to check out **PH7 Équilibre** [21 rue Le Peletier, 9th], an excellent spot run by Claudia and her mother, Murielle, a sophrologist nurse who swears by organic and cruelty-free cooking. The vibrant, colorful interior is full of plants and has a wall covered in drawn flowers. Everything here is developed and concocted to maintain the body's acid-base balance. Among the dishes on offer are L'essentielle, L'alcaliniste and the Grande Soupe Énergisante.

"Being a Parisian is not about being born in Paris, it is about being reborn there."

Sacha Guitry

194A

194B

194C

The Nutrition Counter

196 With their strong values, industrial design, showcasing of local traditions and rare or old types of vegetables, the owners of the concept at the **Causses** nutrition shops come up with a hit in Paris. Good to know: The one in Pigalle has a lovely canteen—open from 11:30 a.m. to 3:00 p.m.—where they serve incredible and affordable salads, bulgur, eggs with watercress mayo and fish with garden zucchini [55 rue Notre-Dame-de-Lorette, 9th].

The Jouffroy Passageway

197 I love all the covered passageways, but the extension of the very hip Passage des Panoramas, **Passage Jouffroy**, is one of my favorites for its authentic, less touristy side. Located west of rue du Faubourg Montmartre, between boulevard Monmartre and rue de la Grange Batelière, this space is flooded with light that shines on the gorgeous tiles throughout the day thanks to the glass roof. There's also a very pretty private reception hall here, **Le Salon des Miroirs** (A) [No. 13], that looks like Versailles with its sublime gilding. **Hôtel Chopin** [No. 46] is at the very end of the passageway and, with its 36 quiet rooms, it's one of the capital's best-kept secrets. Everything is old and nothing has changed in years, but it's the "real" Paris where you can get amazing value for the price if you're looking for a good deal. On the other side of rue de la Grange Batelière, you'll find the entrance to **Passage Verdeau**, well-known for its antique dealers and vintage bookshops. **Holy Bol** [No. 23], an adorable Thai eatery housed in the passage, is also worth the trip.

196

197A

Printemps' Roof

198

You absolutely have to stop in at the luxury department store **Printemps**, if only to marvel at the incredible cupola. My little secret for catching a panoramic view of Paris is located on the top floor (Level 9 of the Beauty and Home building), on cafeteria **Déli-Cieux**'s terrace, where they serve unremarkable sandwiches and salads. That said, you don't necessarily need to order anything to take advantage of the 360-degree view that looks out onto the Madeleine and Opéra on one side, and Église de la Sainte-Trinité (with it's impressive bell tower) and Sacré-Coeur on the other. This spot is surprisingly unknown, so take advantage of the opportunity [64 boulevard Haussmann, 9th].

Gustave Moreau's House

199

I fell in love with this museum located in the house of the famed painter. Unlike in Paris' huge museums, in **Musée National Gustave Moreau** [14 rue de La Rochefoucauld, 9th] there is an almost mystical feel. The floors creak and the walls, covered in countless frames, watercolors and drawings, seem to speak. This house looks like a movie set with its central staircase, cabinets and closets. It's frozen in time and has remained almost intact, in accordance with the wishes of the artist and fine arts professor who invited students to "respect their inner vision" and get off the beaten path.

Appartement de Gustave Moreau

Nombre limité de visiteurs
en raison de la petite
dimension des pièces.

Melissa Unger
Priestess of the soul

→→❧∘₀∘❧←←

200 Melissa Unger was born in the United States to an American father and French mother. Before settling down in Paris, she led the perfect New-York life: she had a golden career, money and lots of success. "I grew up in a well-off socio-economic environment. I worked in the film industry and assisted Robert De Niro and Daniel Day-Lewis, a total stereotype! I was super stressed, overbooked and a bit crazy, but I didn't realize how stressed out I was because it was the only life I knew," she recounts.

Her father died in 2000 after a prolonged illness. This was the catalyst that drove Melissa Unger to take a step back. "After my father's death, I could feel that something was wrong. I really loved my work, but I'd become a workaholic. It was a total addiction that I used to run away from my emotions because they

were too hard to deal with. But I wasn't aware of all that at the time. I thought I was doing well, but I was actually completely asleep," she says.

She quit her job as vice president of an advertising agency to move to her grandmother's house in France. She didn't know anyone in Paris and lost her bearings. She had no job, no phone, no responsibilities or obligations. "I was suddenly in the moment, facing myself, surrounded by emptiness and observation. Without realizing it, I set a meditative state in motion. I sat down at a bistro table and started writing. At that moment, something unique happened, I saw myself writing. It was the first time I saw things from outside myself. In meditation, we call it the 'objective observer.' However, at the time, I had no knowledge of meditation or spirituality."

That moment was a shock that changed her life. Engaged in slow personal progress tied to her childhood, she spent eight years trying to understand what had happened to her. She tells this personal story to explain her **Seymour +** [41 boulevard de Magenta, 10th] concept, a "spa for the spirit" located in a space cut off from technology and the outside world where you can reconnect with yourself. "Seymour + was born out of my psychological quest where I used myself as a guinea pig and did a lot of cleaning house. It's a five-step path. 'Cutting out all technology and contact with the outside world': that was me arriving in Paris, far from all social and familial pressures. 'Looking at yourself in the mirror': that was me asking myself who I really am. I won't go into everything that comes afterward, but it's a quest and a real meeting with the self."

While Seymour + place attracts philosophers who want to talk about consciousness, spirituality and energy, others are simply looking for spiritual relaxation or a fun experience. Others may also be at a turning point in their lives and come to Seymour + to be alone with themselves. "It's a very big, luminous space, and it costs only €7. Each person goes through the experience differently. I built this project and the project built me. Seymour was my father's name."

Her favorite spot in the neighborhood? **Les Douches** [5 rue Legouvé, 10th], a secret art gallery built in an old public shower house. Also, she suggests taking a walk down **rue Sainte-Marthe** [10th], a real gem, and visiting **La Piñata** [25 rue des Vinaigriers, 10th], a store that sells the essentials for a Latin American fiesta: Nothing lifts the spirit quite like partying in a small Parisian apartment!

Yummy Burgers in the Faubourg

201 Entirely decorated with an Empire-inspired, retro, chic decor, the bistro **Le Napoléon** [73 rue du Faubourg Saint-Denis, 10th] is a neighborhood standard, for its sunny terrace. You can order good food from their typical Parisian bistro menu that includes excellent burgers. Reserve a booth at the very back for groups of eight. If you like burgers, **Mamie Burger** [No. 75]—a new concept that Parisians have pounced on—is right next door. A bit farther, **Paris New York** [No. 50] is also one of the best destinations for burgers and fries in Paris. A small tip: Avoid the slightly sketchy **Château d'Eau Metro** station.

202 C

202 B

URFA DURUM
CHEZ SELAM

SANDWICH TRADITIONNEL KURDE

202 A

52 FAUBOURG SAINT DENIS

Saint-Denis' Neo-Faubourg

202

A new go-to for young, hip Parisians, rue du Faubourg Saint-Denis (A) [10th Arrondissement] is changing quickly. While the area is full of Pakistani and Indian influences, there's also an overlap with boho Paris and the city's more popular northern arrondissements, offering the best of both worlds. On one side, you could go to the high-design, minimalist decor restaurant **52** [No. 52] to eat crunchy maki rolls, sea bream carpaccio or chicken. On the other, you might go for Kurdish pita at the hole-in-the-wall **Urfa Dürüm** (B) [No. 58], where you can take a break on one of the terrace's short stools. Men in suits rub shoulders with the neighborhood's multiethnic youth. For a drink, try the quasi-clandestine **Le Syndicat** [No. 51] cocktail club hidden behind a door covered in graffiti. **Floyd's** (C) [11 rue d'Enghien, 10th] isn't much to look at from the street, but it's well known for excellent grilled meat. It's a wonderful restaurant with a raw wood decor dining room at the very end of the hallway, but shh! It's a secret.

Hotel Love

203

Finding true love on rue de la Fidélité? Now there's something to dream about! Opened on November 23, 2015, 10 days after the Paris terrorist attacks, **Hôtel Grand Amour** (A) [18 rue de la Fidélité, 10th] suffered during the days following the sad events, but has since become the neighborhood's new hot spot. It belongs to the same owners as **Hôtel Amour** [8 rue de Navarin, 9th]. Take a seat on their small, heated terrace or indoors in the restaurant section. The vibe is romantic, and lounge music sets the tone. Order a bulgur risotto or small roasted sole, followed by cheese from Laurent Dubois. The hotel has 42 small, medium and large rooms, as well as an apartment.

A Greenery Palace

204

I fell in love with **La Fidelité** [12 rue de la Fidélité, 10th], a chic, plant-filled brasserie designed as a refreshing space where you can recharge your batteries. Drink a delicious cocktail at the long black marble bar or take a seat at a jungle-green booth that matches the big tropical plants. Taste their bistronomy cuisine beneath palace-worthy chandeliers: It's all very unusual for the area.

203 A

The Ayurveda Hideout

205 Nicknamed "Little Islamabad," Passage Brady is well known and included in many guidebooks for its Pakistani and Indian restaurants. The area isn't all that interesting in my opinion, except for a tiny ayurveda pharmacy, **Velan**, at the very end of the passageway. The name travels by word of mouth, and this place is a gold mine for natural Indian products, teas and medicinal herbs to balance your chakra and restore vital energy. Buy raw, non-refined shea butter, plant-based dye or a natural powder to make yourself a face mask at home. You'd be surprised to see how many people cross the threshold of this micro ayurveda institution [83-87 Passage Brady, 10th].

A Walk Along the Canal

206 **Canal Saint-Martin** is the perfect spot to wander around on a sunny day. Cross the small footbridges (A) and walk leisurely along the canal. Have your morning coffee at **Rachel's sur le Canal** [72 quai de Jemmapes, 10th]. She's the cheesecake high-priestess who just opened a new location in eastern Paris. Cross the canal by taking the small footbridge at the corner of avenue Richerand, and you'll find yourself on quai de Valmy that's home to the must-try restaurant **Chez Prune** [36 rue Beaurepaire, 10th]. This spot with a legendary terrace serves as the headquarters for the neighborhood's first boho residents. Check out the **Artazart** [83 quai de Valmy, 10th] design bookshop or grab a sandwich at **Du Pain et Des Idées** [34 rue Yves Toudic, 10th], a fine bakery built in 1870 that's registered as a historical monument. In the evening, **Hôtel du Nord** (B) [102 quai de Jemmapes, 10th]—with decor inspired by Marcel Carné's film *Hôtel du Nord*—is the go-to elegant bistro for a romantic, candlelit meal.

206 A

Marseille Street Outlets

207 While the canal is becoming gentrified, there are still many small shops where you'll find deals. To the great delight of fashionistas, rue de Marseille is a designer outlet paradise where you can take advantage of huge markdowns on retail prices. You'll find **Stock Maje** [No. 4], **Stock Claudie Pierlot** [No. 6] and **Stock Les Petites** [No. 11], as well as many clothing boutiques. After your shopping spree, grab a bite at **Mems** [No. 1], a modern and quirky bistro with a lovely, sunny terrace, run by David and his sister, Deborah.

206 B

208

Alternative Brunch

208 Here's *the* place to go to with friends on Sunday afternoons. The furniture is old, scuffed and ripped, and the vibe is hodgepodge. It feels like a movie set, which is a surprisingly enjoyable sensation. You'll be dreamily transported by the music. On the second floor, there's a bookstore, full of hidden gems like *The Diary of Anne Frank*. With old books, antiques and vintage clothing, **Le Comptoir Général** [80 Quai de Jemmapes, 10th] is a secondhand store, museum, bar, cinema and restaurant—all in one. It's the type of gathering place that's hard to come by and conveys fraternity. Their motto is "promote the emergence of a new united, responsible and open language that's curious about other places and ways of life." Try their signature Secousse cocktail made with hibiscus juice and rum.

Sleeping in the Eastern Part of Town

209 Located behind Porte Saint-Martin, **Hôtel Providence** [90 rue René Boulanger, 10th] is the new east-end destination. The 1854 building has 18 rooms, including a 40-square-meter (431-square-foot) suite with a breathtaking view of Paris' rooftops. You can even see Sacré-Coeur as you soak in the tub. It's also an excellent winter spot for a cocktail by the fireplace.

"Whoever does not visit Paris regularly will never truly be elegant."

Honoré de Balzac

Institut de Bonté

210 If you visit only one establishment on quai de Jemmapes, it should be this one. **Institut de Bonté** [84 quai de Jemmapes, 10th] is a trip, where you'll find whole items, a hop into a country setting with a fruit and vegetable merchant. As soon as you set foot inside, you'll find baskets of carrots, cucumbers, beets and fresh herbs. Untreated wood has been used throughout. Take a seat at the counter facing the bay window to watch the sun reflect off Canal Saint-Martin, or sit at one of the long wooden tables, so conducive to conviviality. Order freshly pressed juice, scented water or organic chocolate cake as you blissfully daydream to the sounds of folk music.

The Picturesque Hippy Street

211 Rue Sainte-Marthe in lower Belleville is an unknown 10th-arrondissement gem. Bohemian and increasingly hip, it will charm you with its cheerful, colorful facades. This is where Paris' working class once lived, which explains the village vibe. The street got a makeover a few years ago, and you'll now find a bunch of small quiet terraces, bi-yearly secondhand sales and occasional concerts. As for food, it's a mixed bag including French, Moroccan, Brazilian, Rwandan and Chilean options. To stay with the funky spirit, stop in at **La Baraque A.** [31 rue Juliette Dodu, 10th], a café and tearoom with lunch and brunch menus, where you can marvel at the colorful, Alice-in-Wonderland-worthy facade.

11th and 12th Arrondissements

BUSTLING and VIBRANT

Stock up on fresh produce at the Marché d'Aligre, soak up the marina atmosphere at the Port de l'Arsenal, enjoy happy hour at Oberkampf, sample the foodie/culinary treasures on rue Paul Bert, and finish up in an out-of-way bar where the nights never end.

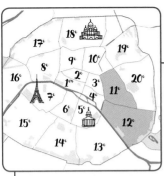

Bustling and Vibrant

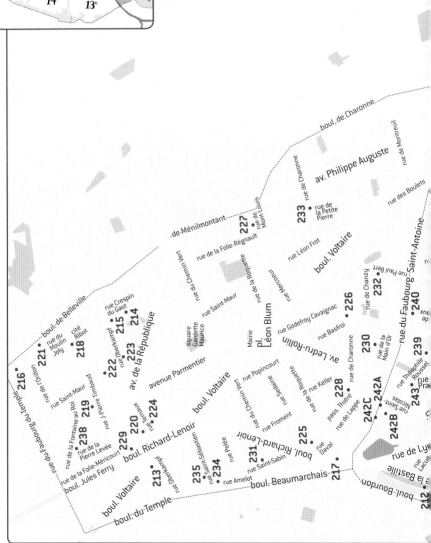

boul. de Charonne

av. Philippe Auguste

rue de Montreuil

rue des Boulets

rue de Charonne

233 • rue de la Petite Pierre

rue de Ménilmontant

rue de Louis Mont-Louis

227 •

rue de la Folie-Régnault

rue Léon Frot

boul. Voltaire

rue de la Roquette

rue du Chemin Vert

rue Saint-Maur

rue Merceour

rue de Chanzy

rue Paul Bert

232 •

rue du Faubourg-Saint-Antoine

240 •

rue Crespin du Gast

rue Oberkampf

215 • 214 •

rue Godefroy Cavaignac

226 •

rue Basfroi

230 •

rue de la Main d'Or

rue Théophile Roussel

239 •

boul. de Belleville

221 •

rue du Moulin Joly

cité Ribot

218 •

222 • 223 •

av. de la République

Square Gardette Maurice

Mairie

pl. Léon Blum

av. Ledru-Rollin

rue de Charonne

228 •

242A •

rue Saint Nicolas

243 •

rue de l'Orillon

216 •

rue Saint-Maur

rue de la Fontaine au Roi

219 •

rue J.-Pierre Timbaud

220 •

rue Ternaux

224 •

avenue Parmentier

boul. Voltaire

rue Popincourt

rue Sedaine

rue de la Roquette

rue Keller

pass. Thiéré

rue de Lappe

242C •

242B •

rue de la Folie-Méricourt

rue de la Pierre Levée

238 •

229 •

boul. Richard-Lenoir

boul. Richard-Lenoir

rue du Chemin Vert

225 •

rue Daval

217 •

rue de Ly

boul. Bourdon

212

boul. Jules Ferry

boul. Voltaire

213 •

rue Oberkampf

235 •

rue Saint-Sébastien

234 •

rue Pelée

rue Amelot

rue Saint-Sabin

231 •

boul. Beaumarchais

la Bastille

boul.-du-Temple

The Arsenal's Port

212 Pontoons, small boats, seagulls and seafood restaurants: Yes, you're still in Paris! For a marina vibe in the heart of the city, stop in at Port de l'Arsenal (also called Bassin de l'Arsenal), just south of Place de la Bastille. It's actually the extension of Canal Saint-Martin, which flows into the Seine. Take a stroll near the garden along the quay, have a quiet picnic by the water or sit on the terrace at **Grand Bleu** [67 boulevard de la Bastille, 12th]. However, it would be ideal to know a boat owner!

Italian-Style *Aperitivo*

213 **Ober Mamma** [107 boulevard Richard Lenoir, 11th] offers up Italian-style *aperitivo* and is one of the Oberkampf area's best destinations. As of 6:00 p.m., you can have a drink at the bar and enjoy free all-you-can-eat Tuscan charcuterie, Parmesan (the wheels are on display) and mozzarella that arrives from Naples every two days. Yum! There's also an excellent trattoria at the back. Dine beneath a lit-up tree next to a double wood-burning oven. Traditional Italian dishes abound in this sublime location with gorgeous 19th-century moldings and a beautiful glass roof. The decor was designed by London's young rising star, Alexander Waterworth.

A Rooftop Bar

214 **Le Perchoir** [14 rue Crespin du Gast, 11th] has one of the hippest elevated terraces in Paris. Get there around 7:30 p.m. for a breathtaking happy hour with a view of surrounding rooftops and Sacré-Coeur in the distance. The wait can be long, so it's a good idea to make dinner reservations. Terrace access is included in the price and everyone has to pay up at the entrance. The fixed-price €50 menu includes mezze appetizers, a main and dessert. Everything is organic and made to share. Feast on vegetable gazpacho with elderberry flowers, fresh oysters, potato chips with cuttlefish ink and ginger beef tartare. The long wait is a small downside, but the view is insane [14 rue Crespin du Gast, 11th].

217

La Môme's Museum

215 "La Vie en Rose" is the internationally recognized song that makes people dream of Paris. At the very beginning of her career, Édith Piaf lived in the Ménilmontant neighborhood. Her old apartment has been turned into a museum where you can listen to sound bites and see all sorts of objects, accessories, photos, letters and clothing that belonged to *La Môme*. Keep in mind that you can only visit the museum by appointment [5 rue Crespin du Gast, 11th].

The Vietnamese Canteen

216 Located right by Belleville Metro, **Dong Huong** [14 rue Louis Bonnet, 11th] is a huge Vietnamese eatery with many rooms. The service is super-fast and it gets packed at night. Stop in for a tasty inexpensive *bun* or, hungover after a night of drinking, for a big bowl of comforting phô. Put it on your itinerary!

De la Bastille Market

217 Every Thursday from 7:00 a.m. to 2:30 p.m. and on Sundays from 7:00 a.m. to 3:00 p.m., the biggest and most eclectic market in central Paris sets up shop on boulevard Richard Lenoir's median strip between Place de la Bastille and rue Saint-Sabin. You'll find clothes, soaps, pashminas, olives, bread, wine, cheese and organic fruits and vegetables. The fishmonger mixes in with artisans and jewelry sellers, making for a jumble of smells, flavors and great finds. It's a must for those who love markets and fresh ingredients [boulevard Richard Lenoir, 11th].

The Scriptwriters' Café

218

Cannibale Café [93 rue Jean-Pierre Timbaud, 11th] is a top destination for the artists, actors and scriptwriters who live in the 11th Arrondissement. The interior has an authentic retro decor, a restaurant area, café, large covered terrace in case it rains and another open one for sunny days. Service is friendly and you can hang around to write your script as you sip on coffee or one of their house specialties: excellent, rich, homemade hot chocolate. Go for the atmosphere rather than the food, or for a DJ night when the "working room" becomes a party zone.

Happy Hour at 11ème Domaine

219

If you like cheese and charcuterie boards accompanied by good wine, **Le 11ème Domaine** [14 rue des Trois Bornes, 11th] wine bar is for you. This place is very Parisian with raw wood, walls lined with bottles and a convivial space where regulars gather to savor private imports and order delicious coppa, dried sausage, runny goat's cheese and fig jam served on slate serving boards. It's the perfect happy hour! On the same street, you should also try the **Les P'tites Indécises** [No. 2] restaurant. With so many windows, it feels like being on an outdoor veranda.

Aux Deux Amis

220 In this festive, sometimes overexcited neighborhood, is a little Franco-Spanish high-end tapas destination that serves absolutely delicious small dishes. It has a great vibe and it's full of stylish people. **Aux Deux Amis** [45 rue Oberkampf, 11ᵗʰ] gets crowded with the area's elite, and even Paris' hip west-enders are happy to make this "faraway" trek for an evening.

Kyobashi

222 This is a real Japanese restaurant with affordable prices. There are many in the neighborhood and all are not created equal, but **Kyobashi** [117 rue Saint-Maur, 11ᵗʰ] is one of the best. They serve a vast array of small appetizers before mains, which is a welcome change from traditional miso soup. It's always a delicious surprise.

The Hippest Of Youth Hostels

221 After having spent 300 nights in youth hostels worldwide, childhood friends Louis, Matthieu and Damien left the consulting and finance industry to open Paris' trendiest youth hostel. Located in Belleville at the 11ᵗʰ Arrondissement's border, **Les Piaules** [59 boulevard de Belleville, 11ᵗʰ] offers quality lodging with a wonderful Kristian Gavoille-designed decor. Catch a panoramic view of Paris from the roof for just €30 a night. There are four rooftop rooms, including a few private ones. Even if you're not staying at the hostel, I highly recommend going to their New-York loft-style bar for happy hour. This place has an international vibe where DJ music sets the tone; it's ideal for meeting people from all over the world.

Happy Hour on Oberkampf Street

223 I love the many happy hour options on rue Oberkampf where you can still find pints of beer and cocktails for under €5, and where almost all the bars have happy hour rates until 10:00 p.m. Head to **Chez Justine** [No. 96] until 9:00 p.m. for a €5 glass of champagne. Musicians can also take advantage of their grand piano. **Café Charbon** [No. 109] has kept its throwback decor, and the walls are covered in cabaret-era paintings. Walk down rue Oberkampf between avenue de la République and boulevard de Belleville to discover small bars with prices to match.

Ternaux Street

224 There are 152 meters (500 feet) between rue de la Folie-Méricourt and rue Neuve Popincourt. This small street section (also called Village Popincourt) is a peaceful contrast to rue Oberkampf's feverish, festive atmosphere. You'll find **Paris Féni** [15 rue Ternaux, 11th], a great healthy restaurant serving Bangladeshi and Indian food, with a menu full of delicious juices. The divine chapati and marinated salmon is fresh, colorful and chock-full of vitamins. Stop in at **Nils Avril** [No. 19], a clothing and accessories boutique with feminine, laid-back and hip pieces. **Ave Maria** [1 rue Jacquard, 11th] right across the street is the perfect place for a happy hour drink or taste of Brazilian specialties. This place will plunge you into a setting far away from Paris with its decor full of Latino Virgin Marys and Hindu goddesses. Also on the pedestrian-only street, **Chambelland** [No. 14] doubles as a small Italian restaurant and bakery with gluten-free bread. This spot is known for its truffle pizza made with Camargue rice flour from the Chambelland mill in the south of France. The establishment on the incredibly charming street belongs to founders Nathaniel Doboin and Thomas Teffri-Chambelland.

The Hidden Bar

225 Places done up like clandestine bars inspired by the Prohibition era have never been as popular in Paris as they are now. Hidden behind the heavy, metal door of what's supposed to be a cold room, **Moonshiner** is a great jazzy bar with low lighting. The facade is home to **Da Vito** pizzeria [5 rue Sedaine, 11th]. I love the suspense and fun, forbidden side.

The Bertrand Grébaut Trio

226 Bertrand Grébaut (trained by Michelin-starred chef Alain Passard) raised rue de Charonne to the ranks of high Parisian bistronomy with **Septime** [No. 80]. Come try their selection of delicious, affordably priced dishes in the company of other like-minded (and well-informed) gourmets. After this establishment's wild success, the celebrity chef opened **Septime La Cave** [3 rue Basfroi, 11th], where they serve excellent natural wines and updated boards for a foodie happy hour. Let's not forget the chef's third restaurant, **Clamato** [80 rue de Charonne, 11th]: It's a fish bar devoted to seafood and shellfish, where dishes are concocted by Canadian chef Érica Archambault, beloved for her famous maple syrup pie.

The Fashion-Forward Photography Studio

227 Paris is one of the world's fashion and haute couture capitals, where the greatest photographers rub shoulders with creative types. Fashion lovers should note that **Le Petit Oiseau Va Sortir** [7 rue de Mont-Louis, 11th] is one of the greatest photography studios in Paris. This is where some of the biggest photo shoots take place, right by Père Lachaise Cemetery. The space, light and lighting are all amazing. I love the private alleyway leading to the studio that feels like a small village, especially when you're aware of all the glamor hidden beyond. For the last few years, the space has organized open house days in November during *Mois de la Photo* (Photography Month). It's a great opportunity to see the backstage of Parisian fashion.

An Urban Art Gallery

229 Raised to the ranks of international art, street art is increasingly shown in galleries. If you find yourself in Paris, keep an eye out for the **Openspace** [116 boulevard Richard Lenoir, 11th] gallery's exhibits; they're the first place to devote themselves to international urban contemporary art. This innovative gallery features historic street art figures, such as Ernest Pignon-Ernest, as well as emerging talent like Levalet.

The Most Rock 'n' Roll Bar

230 A long bar, walls that disappear beneath posters, soft red lighting, candles and a rockabilly crowd: If you're into funky, retro atmospheres, you should consider an evening at **Le Fanfaron** bar [6 rue de la Main d'Or, 11th], a true-blue temple of rock. This place starts to fill up at 7:00 p.m., and they play 1960s oldies hits on repeat, to the great delight of the absolutely wonderful, eclectic Parisian crowd. Elvis, Iggy Pop, Gainsbourg and Dutronc: You're in for good old vinyl and reasonably priced cocktails.

Artisanal Boots

228 Parisians have great respect for traditional and artisanal know-how. **La Botte Gardiane** [25 rue de Charonne, 11th] is a Paris classic. This brand from Camargue became successful thanks to their classic Gardiane boot, a slightly Western leather design that's entirely handmade. You'll also find a lovely selection of sandals and all sorts of accessories. The brand's first boutique is in the 11th Arrondissement, but there's also a second one in the Marais [25 rue du Bourg Tibourg, 4th].

The Perfect Laid-Back Italian Eatery

231 Italian restaurant **Amici Miei** [44 rue Saint-Sabin, 11th] makes the people on this street very happy and has become a fave of mine. Their pizza is delicious and the authentic decor is modern, laid-back and unpretentious. In short, it's a good weekday eatery, and you should get there early.

Foodie Street

232

While rue du Nil has its Frenchie and rue de Charonne its Septime, rue Paul Bert has it's clutch of elite gourmet restaurants, thanks to chef Bertrand Auboyneau. First, there's **Le Bistrot Paul Bert** (A) [18 rue Paul Bert, 11th] for a classic rib steak and fries. Then there are **L'Écailler du Bistrot** [No. 22], which focuses mainly on seafood and **6 Paul Bert** [No. 6], which is more modern and serves a selection of reinvented bistronomy-style dishes. Finally, there's **La Cave** (B) [No. 16], which has excellent natural wines and small dishes cooked up by Canadian chef Louis-Philippe Riel (former chef at 6 Paul Bert). People who love cooking should stop in at **La Cocotte** [No. 5] boutique to see their latest selection of trendy kitchenware.

Ping-Pong at Square Colbert

233

If you're on rue de Charonne, go to No. 159 and open the gate. Square Colbert is gorgeous and unknown because it's almost unfindable, hidden in the courtyard of an 18th-century mansion hotel that was once a medical boarding home. It's a good spot for a quiet picnic, to play outdoor ping-pong or kick back with a good book. It's also a great destination if you have kids, since the park has a play area and little garden (Jardin Marcotte), where they host free gardening workshops [159 rue de Charonne, 11th].

LE BISTROT PAUL BERT

232 A

232 B

Cave Paul Bert

235

Les Jardins du Marais Hotel

234 This extremely charming hotel is very well located and hidden behinde its facade is one of the largest open-air terraces in Paris. The 1,500–square-meter (16,146-square-foot) sun-drenched, paved courtyard is a peaceful haven away from Paris' effervescence. **Les Jardins du Marais** hotel [74 rue Amelot, 11th] occasionally hosts outdoor yoga beneath a gorgeous glass roof.

An Entrenched Bistro

235 Located on a quiet street, **Au Passage** [1 bis Passage Saint-Sébastien, 11th], the so-called local squatter bar, has all the charm of a tapas bar and village inn. They serve excellent, small bistronomy-style market dishes in a simple setting. The menu is written out on a large blackboard and includes a dozen or so mini *raciones* (shared plates). Everything at this no-fuss establishment is exquisite with excellent value for the price.

The Real Thing

236 Open every day of the week except Monday, Marché d'Aligre [Place d'Aligre, 12th] is one of the city's most diverse and authentic markets. Farm-fresh ingredients, rotisserie, organic and rare vegetables, carrots that smell like earth, small Jordanian cucumbers, Brazilian lemons, Peruvian mangoes, Turkish pomegranates and Sicilian tomatoes! There are a few secondhand stands set up in the center. Take in the vibe at one of the cafés along the square or go near by to **The Bottle Shop** [5 rue Trousseau, 11th] pub where you can drink pints to the sound of rock 'n' roll. They also serve excellent Sunday brunch.]

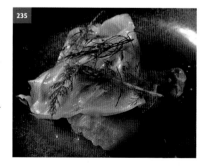

235

A Most Colorful Street

237 In the mood for some lilac purple, apple green or golden yellow? Rain or shine, you can add color to your life by making a detour on **rue Crémieux**, a pedestrian walkway right by Gare de Lyon that's become popular, thanks to its multicolored street fronts. It feels like southern Italy or Notting Hill, and certain facades are even decorated with trees. It's a 144-meter (472-foot) long, sun-filled trip [Rue Crémieux, 12th].

A drink on the Sidewalk

239 It may be tiny, but what an atmosphere! If you're close to Marché d'Aligre, **Le Baron Rouge** [1 rue Théophile Roussel, 12th] is a must for a festive happy hour. Drink a good vintage wine, and taste some oysters and terroir charcuterie or cheese boards in a welcoming, quintessentially Parisian setting. If you can't get a table inside, chat on the sidewalk, in keeping with tradition.

The Zen Vegan Canteen

238 At health haven **Soya** [20 rue de la Pierre Levée, 11th], everything is 99-percent organic, vegan and gluten-free. It's a delight for vegetarians, who can indulge in the varied, delicious menu in an urban, industrial loft-style setting. In the evening, the wooden tables are lit with pretty candles. Mezze to share, plant-based caviar, fresh seaweed tartare, big salads and gluten-free salted caramel and chocolate delights are all in store.

The Neighborhood's Sure Bet

240 "Another bistro," you might say to yourself, but **L'Ébauchoir** [43-45 rue de Cîteaux, 12th] is a 12th-Arrondissement icon! With its black-and-white checkerboard tiles, mirrors, frescoes of old Paris on the walls and close-set wooden tables, it's a sure bet that's both welcoming and elegant. Enjoy their delicious seared foie gras, oyster ceviche or wild Normand hake on a wonderful, quiet summertime terrace.

241

A Walk Along Coulée Verte

241 Located on an old train track, **Coulée Verte René-Dumont** makes for a beautiful nature walk that starts at Place de la Bastille and goes all the way to Square Charles Péguy. This is your chance to visit the 11th and 12th Arrondissements while doing something active. Start the hike at Opéra Bastille and walk down rue de Lyon before going up the stairs on your left at the parking entrance. You'll find yourself high up on the des Arts overpass, emblematic of the 12th Arrondissement's scenery with its vaults and huge glass roofs. It's also home to a bunch of small artist workshops at the rue Daumesnil level. In the summer, the path fills with wonderful flowers and lush vegetation. You'll also cross a lovely bridge that goes over boulevard Diderot. Continue your walk all the way up to rue Montgallet and take the footbridge that overlooks Jardin de Reuilly. It's a sea of greenery for a breath of fresh air.

The Secrets of Faubourg Saint-Antoine

242 I love wandering around **rue du Faubourg Saint-Antoine** (A), where there's a bunch of accessible shops with a popular, lively vibe. **Passage du Chantier** (B) is hidden at the very heart of all this excitement. The paved alleyway is frozen in time, devoted to woodworking crafts, and full of signs and courtyards. It's a lovely, timeless break where bloggers love to take photos of themselves to show a more authentic side of Paris. Farther down rue du Faubourg Saint-Antoine, you'll find **L'Arbre à Lettres** (C) [62 rue du Faubourg Saint-Antoine, 12th] bookstore that has an amazing selection of French literary works. Make time for the children's section that's flooded with light, thanks to huge bay windows that look out onto a lovely yard lined with vines at what used to be the site of an old mansion hotel.

242 B

A True-Blue Bastille Designer

243 Nathalie Dumeix is the name of a true fashionista, as well as of a one hundred percent Parisian brand that has only one shop, here, in the heart of the Bastille neighborhood. All items are made in France, and you'll find pretty cardigans, sweaters and dresses to create a very Birkin look that blends perfectly with French chic and laid-back elegance [10 rue Théophile Roussel, 12th].

A Children's Restaurant

244 Séverine Haïat and Élisabeth Conter created this place that all parents dream about. Located on the Cinémathèque Française's premises, **Les 400 Coups** [51 rue de Bercy, 12th] is a café-restaurant that offers (on weekends only) a kid-adapted menu and huge play area with screens, shadow puppets and books. Highchairs are available and, in the summer, there's a big terrace where you can soak up the sun. This place is open to adults throughout the week, and it's an excellent destination to combine a good meal with a film at the Cinémathèque.

→→→→→ ★ ←←←←←

MONTMARTRE
and
BATIGNOLLES

Mount the impressive staircase to the Sacré-
Cœur basilica, meander in the vineyard at Clos
Montmartre, wander through Place des Abbesses,
relive the Dada moment close to Ternes, savor
the exquisite pastry at Aux Merveilleux de Fred,
get your groceries on rue de Lévis and surrender
to the charming atmosphere of the Batignolles
neighborhood.

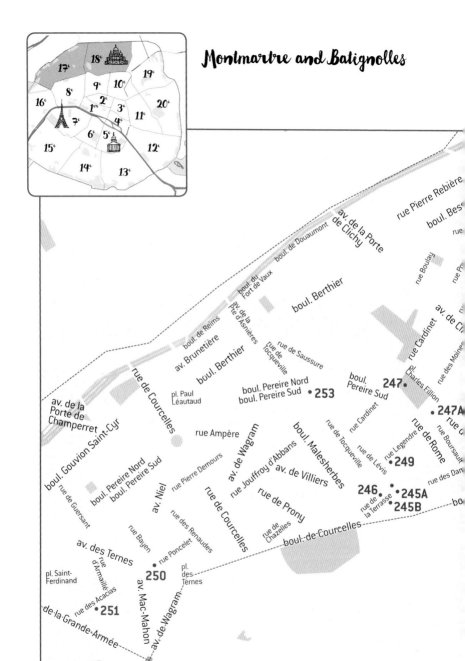

Montmartre and Balignolles

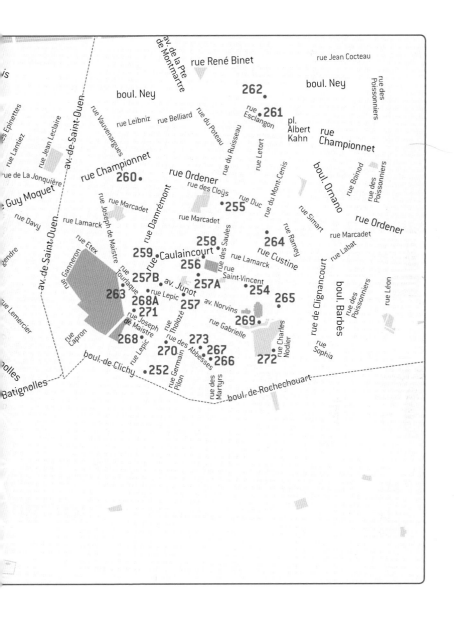

rue René Binet

rue Jean Cocteau

boul. Ney

boul. Ney

262

rue Esclangon 261

pl. Albert Kahn

rue Championnet

rue des Épinettes

rue Lantiez

rue Jean Leclaire

av.-de-Saint-Ouen

rue Vauvenargues

rue Leibniz

rue Belliard

rue du Poteau

rue du Ruisseau

rue Letort

rue des Poissonniers

Guy Moquet

rue de La Jonquière

rue Championnet

260

rue Ordener

rue des Cloÿs

rue Duc

rue du Mont-Cenis

boul. Ornano

rue Boinod

rue des Poissonniers

rue Davy

rue Lamarck

rue Marcadet

rue Joseph de Maistre

rue Damrémont

rue Marcadet

255

rue Simart

rue Ordener

rue Marcadet

gendre

av.-de-Saint-Ouen

rue Etex

rue Ganneron

258

259 •Caulaincourt

256

rue des Saules

264

rue Ramey

rue Custine

rue Lamarck

rue Labat

rue Léon

rue Tourlaque

257B

av. Junot

257A

rue Saint-Vincent

254

265

boul. Barbès

rue des Poissonniers

rue Lemercier

263

rue Lepic

268A

257

av. Norvins

271

rue Tholozé

269

rue de Clignancourt

252

268

rue Lepic

270

rue des Abbesses

273

267

266

272

rue Charles Nodier

rue Sophia

olles

Batignolles

boul.-de-Clichy

rue Joseph de Maistre

rue Capron

rue Germain Pilon

rue des Martyrs

boul.-de-Rochechouart

RESTAURANT *Brigitte*

245 A | 245 B | 245

De Lévis Street

245 Small **rue de Lévis** (A) is one of my favorites for its authentic side. It's also pedestrian-only between boulevard des Batignolles and rue Legendre. You'll find a few fruit sellers, a rotisserie, cheesemonger, bakery, bookshop and a few clothing boutiques. In short, it has everything that makes small shopping streets like this charming. Parisians come here to sit and enjoy a cup of coffee at **Village Café** [22 rue de la Terrasse, 17th]. In the winter, the street is decorated with pretty lights. For a bite to eat, head to **Brigitte** (B) [16 avenue de Villiers, 17th], a welcoming French bistro with a great vibe, loyal clientele and a lovely summertime terrace. You'll be greeted by the owner Charles-Henri Poisson, and his smile.

The Incredible Merveilleux

246 Unthinkable, incredible, revolutionary, eccentric and magnificent! If you're looking to buy dessert for a dinner party, this is the cake you want. Nothing is more deliciously hip than the **Aux Merveilleux de Fred** pastry shop [7 rue de Tocqueville, 17th]. Over the holidays, there will be a long wait to get your hands on a "Merveilleux." This success story goes back to 1982 when Frédéric Vaucamps (Fred) opened his first artisanal pastry shop in Vieux-Lille. His specialty was the meringue mix covered in whipped cream: a traditional pastry from northern France and Flanders. He now has a few shops around Paris, but the one in the 17th Arrondissement at the intersection of rue de Tocqueville and rue de la Terrasse is one of my favorites. Everything is fresh and made right before your eyes. You can buy a whole cake or miniature tasting versions.

246

247

Des Batignolles' Charms

247

The neighborhood nestled between rue de Rome, Saint-Lazare's railroad tracks, avenue de Clichy, rue Cardinet and boulevard des Batignolles is called **Quartier des Batignolles**. This emerging neighborhood is at once boho, artsy, family-focused and residential. To soak in the Batignolles spirit, eat at **L'Endroit** (A) [67 Place du Docteur Félix Lobligeois, 17th] or on one of the square's pretty terraces. **Marché Biologique des Batignolles** (B) [boulevard des Batignolles, on the median strip between No. 27 and No. 35 in the 8th Arrondissement, and between No. 34 and No. 48 in the 17th Arrondissement] is open on Saturdays from 9:00 a.m. to 3:00 p.m. and is full of one hundred percent organic products. For a quiet break, **Square des Batignolles** [147 rue Cardinet, 17th] was designed as an English garden with a grotto, river, waterfall and pool where birds come for a drink of water.

247 A

247 B

Romano Ricci
The romantic in a dapper fedora

248 Romano Ricci is the great-grandson of the illustrious fashion designer Nina Ricci. His grandfather Robert Ricci, created the legendary perfume L'Air du Temps. In 2007, drawing on his own fragrance sensibility as well as his rich heritage, Romano launched his own perfume brand, Juliette Has a Gun, for young, modern romantics. "The character of the fragrance is about having a romantic side, the Juliette who is looking for the man of her dreams, and, on the other hand, the Gun, which destroys all that. The little devil that says, 'There is so much to experience in the world...don't stop now!' "His perfumes, which linger with a presence both distinctive and very intense, are now sold all around the world.

When not traveling, Romano Ricci remains a true Parisian. "I love Paris. It's a city with a soul. It's always hard to explain, but I continue to be fascinated by its beauty, its monuments. They really did a great job renovating them. It's also a remarkably clean city—I really see the difference when I travel abroad. And the women are pretty, and have taste, and the food is good. That's all I need, really!"

With a little luck, you might see Romano eating breakfast in the 17th arrondissement, where he works, or in the 8th, nearby. His favorite Parisian bistro is **Les Gourmets des Ternes** [87 boulevard de Courcelles, 8th], because, according to him, it serves "the best meat *ever*!" The perfumer is never seen without his black fedora, adorned with a beautiful red, white, or purple grosgrain ribbon. All his hats come from **Motsch** [42 avenue George V, 8th], a famous brand founded by Ernest Motsch, and later bought by Hermès. "They aren't made to measure, but I add a large ribbon around them, which is tailored for me." Romano Ricci is a mysterious dandy, refined foodie, and lover of Parisian nights and intimate evenings with his close-knit circle of friends. He's also one of the most endearing people I know. What's his favorite spot in Paris? "**Caviar Kaspia** [17 Place de la Madeleine, 8th]. I love the ambience and I'm crazy about the potatoes Vladivostok, which is one of their specialties."

250 A 250 B

Mitterrand's Bistro

249 **Chez Léon** [32 rue Legendre, 17th] has been a legendary spot since 1934 and has had the likes of French Presidents Charles de Gaulle, Georges Pompidou and François Mitterand walk through its doors. Both passionate about fresh, terroir products, owners Victor and Julien took over this place and transformed it into a real Parisian brasserie. Try their amazing confit octopus carpaccio or the €16 lunch menu for smaller budgets.

249

Dada

250 Every Parisian has, at one time or another, had a lengthy discussion on the terrace of **Dada** (A) [12 avenue des Ternes, 17th] during a festive happy hour, where rosé wine flows freely. The terrace gets packed as soon as the season's first rays of sun shine. I also like rue Poncelet's village feel on the corner, home to one of Paris' most beautiful markets. Among the merchants here, note the **Alléosse** [13 rue Poncelet, 17th] cheese shop where the passion for aging cheese is passed down from father to son. **Maison Pou** (B) [16 avenue des Ternes, 17th] is an institution that was established in 1830, where you can buy incredible crusted pâté, puff pastry and foie gras. The nearby **Église Saint-Ferdinand-des-Ternes** [27 rue d'Armaillé, 17th] is a church worth the trip for its neo-Byzantine style.

Le Crabe Marteau

251 Bang! Bang! Bang! What's that? It's the sound of the crab-cracking mallet in the hands of your table neighbors at **Le Crabe Marteau** [16 rue des Acacias, 17th]. Watch them pick apart the claws and joints of the precious shellfish caught off the Brittany coast and delivered here the same morning. Dungeness, common or spider crab are the house specialties, depending on the season. Your neighbors will enjoy them so much that they'll lick their fingers before throwing the carcasses into the garbage provided for this purpose. Slurp up a deep-shelled, perfectly salty oyster before taking your swing with the mallet. You'll hesitate, start with a shy little bang and miss. Raise it again with more vigor. BANG! It'll spray everywhere. Ahh! Thank god for the big bibs that keep shirts and little black dresses clean!

On the of Le Chat Noir

252 The Chat Noir (black cat) is Montmartre's mascot, and you'll see famous posters of the legendary cat exhibited everywhere on the hill. **Le Chat Noir**, one of Paris' most famous cabarets at the end of the 19th century, has been located at different spots in Montmartre. It started out at 84 Boulevard Rochechouart [18th], moved on to 12 rue Laval (now rue Victor Massé, 9th) and finally landed at 68 Boulevard de Clichy, 8th. As the story goes, the cabaret's owner, Rodolphe Salis, named his establishment Chat Noir as homage to the meowing cat he heard on the night he visited the abandoned space. The *Le Chat Noir* publication came out of the cabaret and notably featured writings by Guy de Maupassant and Victor Hugo, along with Théophile-Alexandre Steinlen's famous illustrations that can now be seen everywhere in Montmartre.

Hotel Gaston

253 At the very end of rue de Tocqueville near Batignolles, you'll find this creative hotel that called upon the **La Splendens Factory** art collective for the design of their common areas. You'll therefore see drawings, quotes and book passages painted on the doors and walls. The rooms are modern and each one is different, while remaining cozy and very comfortable. In short, it's the perfect compromise for a contemporary and stylish atmosphere that's chic without being too stuffy. You won't spend a fortune there either. It might not be the most centrally located hotel, but the area is quiet, residential and safe [51 boulevard Pereire, 17th].

Montmartre's Vines

254 The gorgeous **Clos Montmartre** (A) grapevine plantation is at the corner of rue des Saules and rue Saint-Vincent [18th], and the vintage it produces belongs to the city. If you're in Paris during the second weekend of October, don't miss the Fête des Vendanges de Montmartre (Montmartre grape harvesting festival). Take this opportunity to visit **Musée de Montmartre** [12 rue Cortot, 18th] in an amazing 17th-century residence, a section of which looks out onto the vines. Discover the Paris of Picasso, Renoir, Toulouse-Lautrec and other great artists who lived in the neighborhood and get inspired by its bohemian spirit and unique light.

254A

The Best Pizza

255

Distinguished by its wooden facade and old-fashioned look, **Il Brigante** [14 rue du Ruisseau, 18th] is a cozy pizzeria that smells of real Italian food. Here, owner Salvatore Rototori and his associate Domenico knee the authentic dough right before your eyes. Order the Mortazza topped with fior di latte and ricotta di bufala cheese, mushrooms, arugula, Grana Padano shavings and black truffle mortadella: eat it at one of the long convivial tables inside or in the hallway. Forget everything else for a minute. Take a bite, smile: It's Italy in Paris.

Good Organic Tea

256

François Parent, a diplomat's son, lived all over the world before developing a passion for very high-quality tea. In his **Bonthés & Bio** [98 rue Caulaincourt, 18th] teashop, you'll find incredible organic tea blends developed in partnership with a team of flavorists. Try Un Thé à Tanger (orange blossom-flavored green tea), Formule Magique (grapefruit, passion fruit and vanilla) or their signature tea, Bon Thé (vine peach, red berries and dates). They come packaged in small boxes that are hand-painted by artist Marie Gorlicki. It's the ideal gift to slip into your suitcase.

Junot Avenue

257 In my opinion, the area behind Sacré-Coeur is the most interesting part of Montmartre. Far from Place du Tertre's touristy bustle—a destination for many artist and portrait painters—**Place Dalida** (A) [18th] is one of the more picturesque squares I've seen. It's at the intersection of two cobblestone streets, a staircase and hidden path. Take the small passageway on the right and walk to avenue Junot. Sit down to brunch at **Marcel** [1 Villa Léandre, 18th], an ultra-hip spot that's very sought-after for its modern New York vibe and pretty summertime terrace. Take this opportunity to see the houses at **Villa Léandre**, one of the most beautiful of its kind in Paris. Later on, a cocktail at the chic **Hôtel Particulier** [23 Avenue Junot, Pavillon D] with a gorgeous hidden garden is in order. At the top of avenue Junot, you'll find **Ciné 13 Théâtre** [No. 1], a tiny viewing room with 120 seats that's entirely decorated in 1920s style. The once legendary popular cabaret, **Moulin de la Galette** (B) [No. 3], is now closed to the public. Almost unknown to tourists, rue Norvins is an extension of avenue Junot that leads to the famed Place du Tertre.

The Hope Café

258 This hipster bistro serves one hundred percent organic food in a setting full of skateboards and fresh vegetables. The menu is surprisingly varied at **Hope Café**, from vegetarian to Asian, flavored dishes to traditional burgers and Crying Tiger (beef strips with Thai marinade and coriander). "We put together a menu that we would like to find when dining out," explains the owner. Note that vegetarian and vegan dishes are marked with a green dot [64 rue Lamarck, 18th].

The Highest Staircase

259 Montmartre is full of steep stairways that are a part of the scenery. It's the secret to Parisian thinness, since you need darn good cardio to climb them every day! My favorite is at **Square Caulaincourt** [63-65 rue Caulaincourt, 18th]. With its 122 stairs, it's one of the highest. At the top of the stairs is **Caulaincourt Square Hostel** [2 Square Caulaincourt, 18th], a youth hostel for travelers with smaller budgets.

The German Bar

260

Welcome to **Kiez** (pronounced Kiiitz) [24 rue Vauvenargues, 18th], Paris' first *biergarten*. What's a *biergarten*? The German word means "outdoor brewery." At this place, the only one of its kind in Paris, you can enjoy all sorts of German products in a one hundred percent *Deutsch* atmosphere. Berlin's famous currywurst, Hamburg's hamburger, Bavaria's nürnberger, Swabia's spätzle or the legendary wiener schnitzel... It's a real trip and a great find.

An Underground Hot Spot

261

On the other side of Montmartre, by the Saint-Ouen flea market, you'll come across **CO** [15 rue Esclangon, 18th], an out-of-the-ordinary, whimsical spot in an area you wouldn't usually go to, especially not at night. Located on a residential street, CO breaks all the rules and sets up shop where it's not supposed to. Lovers of underground finds will appreciate the eclectic setting where a piano, candles, paintings of Snow White and frames of the Virgin Mary all share the space in perfect disharmony. Enjoy a signature cocktail at the bar (*CO Brasil*) before eating fish-and-chips in the big hall where the decor gleaned from flea markets lends a hodgepodge feel. Leave your tip in the sequined hat or piggy bank provided for this purpose. "Tipping is sexy!" as we say back home.

The REcyclerie

262 Modern, innovative and fashionable, **La REcyclerie** [83 boulevard Ornano, 18th] is located in an old train station that's been transformed into a living space focused on sustainable and ecological development. In the gigantic café-canteen beneath cathedral ceilings, enjoy one hundred percent local and responsible dishes that are often vegetarian, with excellent cocktails on the side. Visit the urban farm with its chickens, garden, beehives, aquaponics system and community garden. Better yet: Every Sunday from 12:00 p.m. to 6:00 p.m., this place transforms into an ephemeral secondhand sale where Parisians go to exchange, barter, sell and empty their closets. It's all steps away from the Porte de Clignancourt flea market if you're into combining two activities.

A Good Italian Eatery

263 After climbing countless steps on Montmartre's hill, what's better than a good Italian restaurant, full of charm and far from the touristy area? **Pulcinella** [17 rue Damrémont, 18th] is welcoming, convivial, not too stuffy, covered in wood and has a huge Italian fresco to put diners into the *dolce vita* spirit. Enjoy very reasonably priced caprese salad, ham, artichokes, Parmesan and linguini with truffle cream, accompanied by a bottle of Tuscan wine. Simply divine.

The Stars' Asian Go-To

264 **Sourire de Saigon** [54 rue du Mont Cenis, 18th] is popular among the entertainment industry. Treat yourself to a trip to Southeast Asia where the hostesses wear traditional garb. I love the friendly vibe and the decor filled with Buddha figures and colorful lanterns. It's a little romantic-bourgeois destination where they serve excellent Asian food flavored with coconut milk, curry, basil and lemongrass. They also have a great selection of vegetarian dishes.

263

265

The Perché Go-To

265 At the very top of rue Lamarck, at the foot of Sacré-Coeur, you'll find **Les Perchés du Chai** [6 rue Lamarck, 18th] owned by Fred (a Canadian) and his associate, Cyrille. They brought this project to fruition as homage to the previous occupant of the location: a Chinese restauranteur at whose table they often ate. Open only in the evening, the restaurant serves home-cooked tapas made with fresh ingredients, alongside a nice, curated selection of wines from small producers. The atmosphere is warm, convivial and authentic. Try their specialty, the Wagyu beef mini-burgers.

The Abbesses' Barista

266 In the mood for a green coffee that's slightly earthy on the nose or very chocolatey? Choose your acidity level at **Cuillier**, Faubourg Saint-Honoré's renowned roaster that has some of the greatest raw blends in the city. Their motto is "from tree to mug, we work with the best coffees in the world." Along with their new Abbesses location [19 rue Yvonne le Tac, 18th], Cuillier has set up shop at Galeries Lafayette [35 boulevard Haussmann, 9th] and in Saint-Germain-des-Prés [68 rue de Grenelle, 7th].

268 A

The Deepest Metro Station

267 Get off at Abbesses Metro station and climb the endless spiraling stairs. You'll feel as if you'll never get out, which will make you smile! It's Paris' deepest stop (36 meters/118 feet below ground level). You'll emerge at **Place des Abbesses** [18th]—one of my favorites—that will immediately pull you into Montmartre's village vibe. From here, go up to Sacré-Coeur on rue Lepic or take a seat on one of the square's terraces. Montmartre is yours for the taking!

Rue Lepic

268 **Rue Lepic** is probably Montmarte's most famous and touristy street thanks to the movie, *Amélie,* and to **Café des 2 Moulins** [No. 15] where many scenes were filmed with Audrey Tautou. The section between boulevard de Clichy and rue des Abbesses is made up of small food stores, chocolate shops, bakeries and florists in a small, hilly village atmosphere. Most of the restaurants, bars and cafés are very touristy. For brunch, go to **Pain Quotidien** [No. 31] at the corner of rue des Abbesses. Go up rue Lepic and order the Croq'Homard at **Jeanne B** (A) [No. 61]. Right by rue Lepic, you'll find **Le Café Qui Parle** [24 rue Caulaincourt, 18th], another great spot with good quality for the price during brunch and a beautiful terrace.

A Sublime Panoramic View

269 The view from **Escaliers du Sacré-Cœur** [18th], at the very top of Square Louise Michel, is absolutely sublime. Enjoy the pleasant atmosphere created by musicians, couples, giant telescopes and Paris' most iconic monument, which will probably end up in the background of your vacation photo. Take rue Saint-Éleuthère to Square Nadar to catch the only real elevated panoramic perspective of the city. Once there, you can not only see the Eiffel Tower, but you may be able to catch sight of the sun setting over.

269

A Chic Vintage Spot

270 Both owners here are passionate about vintage, so they decided to create **Rose Bunker** [10 rue Aristide Bruant, 18th], a concept store full of little vintage gems found here and there. From the decoration to the unusual objects, the spirit of recycling is set front and center here so you can reinvent your style in a chic, vintage spirit.

View Over Rooftops

271 High up in Montmartre, the **Terrass' Hôtel** [12-14 rue Joseph de Maistre, 18th] has been an artist go-to since 1911, and it has just finished being renovated in 2015. Since then, this place has become a hip destination for travelers, as well as Parisians. Go up to the 7th floor to step into the restaurant, which has an unforgettable view of Paris' rooftops and the Eiffel Tower. In the summer, the terrace transforms into the perfect spot to catch a 180-degree view of Paris' most beautiful monuments, including Les Invalides and Grand Palais. The four-star hotel has 85 rooms and seven suites.

Halle Saint Pierre

272 At the foot of Montmartre's hill, this unusual art gallery is housed in an old market. It's a real temple to non-conformist creativity, which attracts many of Paris' emerging contemporary artists. The high ceilings are incredible and the space is flooded with light, thanks to the huge glass roof. It's a tearoom, bookstore and exhibition room all in one. In short, enough for you to forget about time and wander around for part of the day [2 rue Ronsard, 18th].

The "I Love You" Wall

273 Because Paris has the reputation of being the most romantic city in the world, make a detour to see the wall covered in 311 "I Love Yous" written in 280 languages. This piece, designed by Frédéric Baron and Claire Kito, is a monument devoted to love. It's located in a delightful square with benches for couples, of course. You can never know too many ways to say "I love you" [Square Jehan Rictus, 18th].

19th and 20th Arrondissements

——>>>>★<<<<——

BELLEVILLE
and its
MAGICAL VISTAS

——>>>>★<<<<——

Feast on the terrace at Moncœur Belleville, hunt
for bargains at the best flea markets in Gambetta,
stroll along the banks of the Canal de l'Ourcq,
soak up the Marché de Belleville's cosmopolitan
atmosphere, lounge in the Parc des Buttes-
Chaumont, explore Jourdain village and get a feel
for the vitality of the Paris of the future.

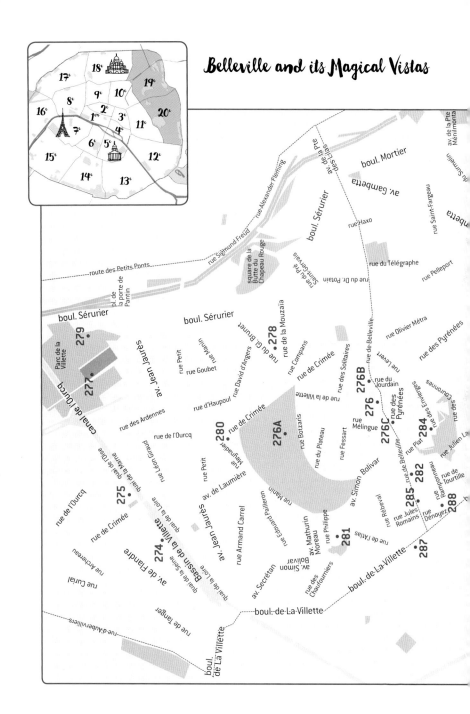

Belleville and its Magical Vistas

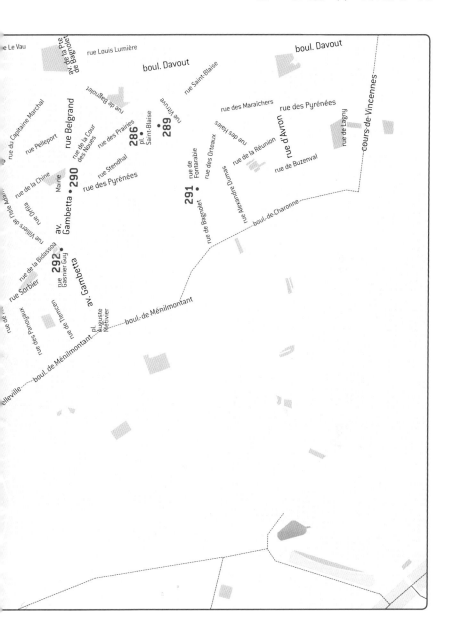

rue Le Vau

av. de la Pte de Bagnolet

rue Louis Lumière

boul. Davout

boul. Davout

rue Saint-Blaise

rue du Capitaine Marchal

rue Pelleport

rue Belgrand

rue de Bagnolet

rue des Maraîchers

rue des Pyrénées

cours-de-Vincennes

rue de la Cour des Noues

rue des Prairies

rue Stendhal

286 pl. Saint-Blaise

rue Vitruve

289

rue des Orteaux

rue des Haies

rue de la Réunion

rue d'Avron

rue de Lagny

rue de la Chine

Mairie

av. Gambetta **• 290**

rue des Pyrénées

rue de Fontarabie

291

rue de Bagnolet

rue Alexandre Dumas

rue de Buzenval

rue de l'Isle Adam

rue Orfila

rue Villiers de l'Isle Adam

rue de la Bidassoa

292 rue Gasnier Guy

av. Gambetta

boul.-de-Charonne

rue Sorbier

rue de Tlemcen

pl. Auguste Métivier

boul. de Ménilmontant

rue des Panoyaux

boul. de Ménilmontant

Belleville

249

Canal de l'Ourcq's Banks

274 Wander around, enjoy the sunshine and have an afternoon drink by the water. Canal de l'Ourcq is an extension of Bassin de la Villette in the 19th Arrondissement, far from Paris' chic, touristy neighborhoods. It's one of my favorite spots to recharge in the heart of the city. Get off at Stalingrad station (lines 2, 5 and 7) or Jaurès station (lines 2, 5 and 7 as well). Between the two Metro stops, **La Rotonde** [6-8 Place de la Bataille de Stalingrad, 19th] designed by Claude-Nicolas Ledoux is an emblematic monument in the urban landscape, which acts as a restaurant with a large terrace. Go up Bassin de la Villette afterward. The most beautiful house here is **Pavillon des Canaux** [39 quai de la Loire, 19th]. It looks like a mansion hotel and has one of the most beautiful terraces on the canal, as well as a working space for freelancers. A bit farther, **Bar Ourcq** [68 quai de la Loire, 19th] is a gathering spot for the neighborhood's lawn bowlers, and you can rent balls to play on the court across the way. If you're in Paris during the summer, keep in mind that Canal de l'Ourcq hosts the annual FestiWall. It's dedicated to street art and the emerging urban artists who have taken over the area. Visitors can marvel at the works painted along the artists' path by the water. You can also take part in many activities, including small cruises, or rent little electric boats at **Marin d'Eau Douce** [37 quai de la Seine, 19th]. To anchor yourself in the neighborhood, **Péniche Antipode** [55 quai de la Seine, 19th] is a very bohemian floating restaurant where you can go for happy hour and see great live shows. Rue de Crimée's lift bridge is at the very end of the pond. If you keep walking, Canal de l'Ourcq has many surprises in store as it becomes a wonderful, bucolic stream in a natural setting. There's also 30 kilometers (18 ½ miles) of bike paths. It's so much fun!

Levalet
The king of illusionist street art

→》.°。‹‹‹

275 At 28 years old, Charles Levalet is an urban art virtuoso. As I wandered through the city in search of sites to visit, new places and new energy, I found myself deeply compelled by his art. Born in Guadeloupe, Levalet studied art in Strasbourg before taking Paris by storm in 2012. Since then, he has covered the city's walls with his art, which is both humorous and full of meaning. Far from run-of-the-mill graffiti, his ephemeral collages are made with India ink and depict life-size human figures that satirize the absurdity of society. "I try to use these scenes to convey ideas that are open-ended, and that depends on the context. So the message is never the same. For example, I did a piece on the quai de Jemmapes for an interview as part of a news show on TF1. I created an allegorical scene that poked fun at the TV world by showing a diabolical newscaster with Guignol-like characters in the background," the artist explained.

Each of his ideas is inspired by a specific place. "I start by scoping out a place. I take measurements and photos, and then I come up with a concept. I create the drawings in my studio, and then I go back to the site to install them," he explained. "It takes about three or four days to create a piece. That includes coming up with an idea, creating it, and applying it. I like installing in the morning, when there are fewer people around, but it's still pretty lively. I never go back to the site to see what's happened to my work. Each drawing is unique, and exists for a while on the street. After that, it's gone forever."

While Levalet has so far installed over a hundred works, only ten or so ever remain. "Sometimes the city cleans them, or people destroy them, or the weather does." In a city like Paris, where every site is preserved or classified as a historical monument, how do you keep ephemeral street art alive? And—first things first—is it even legal? "I've never had any trouble with the law. I do collage, which is pretty easy to remove, and doesn't damage structures. It's a fairly popular medium in this city, and is becoming increasingly legitimate—so much so that some of the town halls have asked me to create work in particular neighborhoods—especially on the Canal de l'Ourcq, in the 19th Arrondissment, or for a street art fair at Carreau du Temple, in the 3rd Arrondissement."

What are his favorite sites to work with? "I like very historic sites, like the quays near Notre-Dame, because there's so much you can do with historic relics, and also

the more run-down neighborhoods, like the 19th or 20th Arrondissements, where there is also so much to see, but with a totally different vibe. I've also done a lot of work in the 11th Arrondissement. Those are the areas that are more open, where I feel good. I try to find neutral places, ones that haven't already been taken over by other artists, and there are certain arrondissements that I avoid. I would never do anything in the 16th, the 18th, or the 6th, which are really aseptic neighborhoods in Paris." Are there any off-limits sites he dreams of? "If I had time, one day I'd like to work on a bigger project, on a quay, 200 meters (650 feet) long. But no, there's not really anywhere off-limits that I dream of working on. I don't want to collage the Louvre pyramid or the Eiffel Tower!" He used to live in the 13th, but now lives in the 19th. "It's an arrondissement that has a lot of ugly areas that aren't very interesting, but there are also small pockets that are really nice!"

Haut-Belleville and Buttes-Chaumont

276 From rue Belleville, go up rue de la Villette between the Jourdain and Pyrénées Metro stations. This street is thriving, and you'll find shops like **Pollen** [7 rue de la Villette, 19th] ,where they sell a great selection of cute dresses, jewelry and accessories. Across the street, **Résine** [No. 6] is its male counterpart. At the very end with its suspension bridge and elevated view of Paris, is the natural and gigantic **Parc des Buttes-Chaumont** (A) [1 rue Botzaris, 19th]. Outdoor eatery **Rosa Bonheur** [2 avenue de la Cascade in Parc des Buttes-Chaumont, 19th] is located at the top of the Buttes. It becomes a meet-up hot spot as soon as summer arrives, and it's a great happy hour destination. Keep on strolling to discover the authentic ambiance of Jourdain village: its epicenter is **Église Saint-Jean-Baptiste de Belleville** (B) [134 rue de Belleville, 19th]. Have a meal at **Il Posto** (C) [356 rue des Pyrénées, 19th], an excellent Italian restaurant, which reminds me of an industrial loft; the terrace is lovely. Or stop at **Bonjour Vietnam** [6 rue Jean-Baptiste Dumais, 19th], a Vietnamese restaurant one should not miss.

278

278

La Petite Halle

277 Right by Canal de l'Ourcq and Philharmonie is a huge, very modern loft-style space. Order one of their pizzas from the wood-burning oven beneath a huge glass roof flooded with light with an urban New York decor. During the summer, they serve cocktails and grilled pizza in the garden equipped with lounge chairs on the gorgeous lawn. **La Petite Halle** [Parc de la Villette, 211 Avenue Jean Jaurès, 19th] regularly hosts live jazz or electronic music. Get there from Porte de Pantin Metro station and walk along Grande Halle from Galerie de la Villette, all the way to Pavillon Paul Delouvrier. A bit farther, you'll find Librairie du Parc and a few kids' rides.

Mouzaïa's Villas

278 An instant fave! It's not an actual tourist attraction, but still a unique Parisian spot if you want to go for a different kind of stroll among these Parisian villas. Here you'll find small pedestrian pathways lined with pretty houses, flowers and gardens for a country feel that contrasts greatly with Paris' neighborhoods. They were inhabited by working class folk at the end of the 19th century, but nowadays, people pay a pretty penny to live in these villas! There are about a dozen in the miniscule **Mouzaïa** neighborhood (Villa des Lilas, Villa Félix Faure, Villa du Progès, etc.) [around rue de Mouzaïa, Botzaris Metro station, 19th].

A Concert at Philharmonie

279 If you like classical, baroque and jazz music, I highly recommend you spend an evening at Philharmonie. This absolutely incredible hall cost 386 million euros to build and was inaugurated in January 2015 under the direction of renowned architect Jean Nouvel. The acoustics are fantastic and seats are affordable. Along with performance halls, the establishment is also home to Musée de la Musique, where you can see legendary instruments like Chopin's piano or one of Brassens' guitars. It's a must for music lovers [221 avenue Jean Jaurès, 19th].

The Secret Hill

281 **Butte Bergeyre** [76 rue Georges Lardennois, 19th] is a micro-neighborhood with a timeless village vibe. It's like the countryside in Paris and very few people know about this place that's far away from all the busy streets. Head to the top for an amazing view of Montmartre's hill and Sacré-Coeur, especially at sunset. Clos des Chaufourniers is a tiny vineyard located here—one of the capital's little treasures. It's not open to the public. The winery produces about 65 liters (17 gallons) of wine per year. Take this opportunity to visit Bergeyre village with its cobblestone streets and picturesque charm.

The Oldest Bread Oven

280 If you're at the foot of Buttes-Chaumont and feel your stomach rumbling, go to **Boulangerie Véronique Mauclerc** [83 rue de Crimée, 19th], where the facade is registered as a historical monument. The building dates back to the 1920s, and is famous for being one of the last remaining bakeries where bread is cooked in a wood-burning oven (since 1904). Everything is traditional and artisanal here. Be warned: There's no baguette, but rather an excellent selection of organic bread. Try the Mikagui loaf made with chestnut flour and nougatine.

A Belleville Coffee

282 Brûlerie Belleville distributes its freshly roasted coffee to the coolest cafés in town. To test it in the heart of the 20th Arrondissement, head to **Cream** [50 rue de Belleville, 20th], an unpretentious coffee shop with a great laid-back vibe. Enjoy their excellent artisanal coffee surrounded by Belleville's boho crowd.

Electronic DJ Twins

➤➤ ₀°₀ ⬅⬅

283 Dreads, statement hats, leather jackets, shades... Brice and Régis Abby (alias William Wilson Doppelgänger) are handsome, stylish, hip—and identical twins. They have capitalized on their twinship by creating their own mark as a duo in the visual arts and as DJ/producers. "We have always operated as a symbiotic pair, ever since we were small children. That part comes naturally to us, and we've also drawn on this in our visual arts research on the theme of doppelgangers." Every day, Brice and Régis dress the same, in monochrome, yet doubly irresistible. "We choose our outfit by consensus, or morning vote (they laugh). All in black, with a very occasional touch of white." Their niche? Electronic music. "We work in visual arts and music. We're DJs and we also create video installations for launches and openings for luxury industries, like fashion and film." When in Paris, you might run into them at an event, or in the front row at a fashion show.

Their burgeoning creative energy is causing a stir on the Parisian scene. "Paris is waking up after a long sleep, but it's still lively and impudent. You can see a real dynamism, more appropriation of urban space: quays, gardens, rooftops and so on. The 19th Arrondissement is the up-and-coming neighborhood that has been overtaken by working artists. That is where the creative duo set up their studio. "The 19th is in the throes of change, with la Philharmonie (see reason n° 279) and the introduction of Grand Paris. Pantin, adjacent to the 19th, has become a creative space, thanks to the introduction of renowned art galleries, like **Thaddaeus Ropac** [69 avenue du Général Leclerc, Pantin], where you see at contemporary art in a minimalist setting. It's no accident that we set up our art and music studio in this flourishing neighborhood." What are their favorite spots in Paris? **The Asado Club** [11 rue Marie et Louise, 10th], along the Canal Saint-Martin, for casual Argentinian cuisine, like empanadas and BBQ. **Le Comptoir Général** [80 quai de Jemmapes, 10th], an unusual spot featuring African décor by way of a sort of cabinet of curiosities. And **Nüba** [36 quai d'Austerlitz, 13th] (Reason 124), a rooftop with a superb panoramic view, perched atop the Cité de la Mode.

Piat Street's Gems

284 In upper Belleville, at the very end of rue Piat, you'll find a very pleasant café called **Moncoeur Belleville** (A) [1 rue des Envierges, 20th], which opens onto an esplanade. It's at the top of Parc de Belleville with a gorgeous view of Paris. Take a seat on one of the nicest terraces in town. It's little known to Parisians because the neighborhood is quite removed. Every Saturday from 11 a.m. to 2:30 p.m., Arnaud and Hector set up an ephemeral display full of Vendée oysters selling for €1 apiece that can be eaten on the spot or taken to go. Enjoy the oceanic feast with a glass of well-chilled Sancerre to achieve perfection.

Lower Belleville's Grocery

285 Belleville's boho crowd loves Cécile Boussarie, owner of **Fine l'Épicerie** [30 rue de Belleville, 20th], which sells refined products, as well as a wide variety of goods from local producers and wine makers. Brittany heather honey, Bonvalot snail products, Les Saisons de Rosalie jams—white nectarine and basil, Penja pepper, etc. For lunch, pick up a sandwiches, the salad of the day or homemade cake and eat on the premises.

The Saint-Blaise Area

286 I adore the Saint-Blaise neighborhood bordered by boulevard Davout, rue Pyrénées, rue d'Avron and rue Vitruve. I love its flower-filled terraces, gardens and the atmosphere that's both rebellious and authentic. While you're there, visit **Place Édith Piaf** [22 rue de la Py, 20th] and the elevated flowery nooks of this neighborhood that's also called Village de Charonne. The cobblestone alleyways have been protected from urbanization and so this place has kept its a real country feel, especially with the vine-covered houses. Eat and sleep at **Mama Shelter** (A) [109 rue de Bagnolet, 20th], where the 172 rooms were decorated by Philippe Starck. The modern, young, hip, quiet and affordable hotel is located by Petite Ceinture, a defunct iron railway line that's emblematic of Old Paris. It's right across from the European pop-rock scene's temple, **La Flèche d'Or** [102 Bis rue Bagnolet, 20th]. The restaurant is worth the trip, notably for its cuisine developed by Guy Savoy. Their incredibly magical summertime rooftop, with hammocks and ping-pong tables, is also noteworthy.

286 A

286 B

286

The Best Dumplings

287 Madame Yuying—the Chinese dumpling queen—runs the show at **Raviolis Chinois Nord-Est** [11 rue Civiale, 20th]. In this well-known tiny establishment adored by bloggers and dumpling lovers, the creation of this dish has become a high art. Order your dumplings steamed or fried (stuffed with pork, shrimp or vegetables) and sip on Chinese beer as you wait. Everything is homemade and, at 5 € for 10 dumplings, their prices are unbeatable.

A Cosmopolitan Market

288 Every Tuesday and Friday morning, trucks arrive at dawn, loaded with crates of peaches, apricots, melons, cheese, etc. **Marché de Belleville**—Paris' most cosmopolitan market—becomes packed with loyal customers, locals and restaurateurs searching for the freshest and least expensive ingredients available. It's a delicious blend of social diversity [boulevard de Belleville's median strip, Couronnes Metro station (line 2), 20th].

The Panama Wholesaler

289

Parisians are crazy for hats that add style and personality to any outfit, from happy hour at Café Charlot to hyper-hip evenings in Jardins de Bagatelle. Even Diane Kruger wears one to Roland-Garros in the scorching heat, paired with sunglasses and messy side-swept hair; it's written into the Parisian genetic code. People of course buy them for strolling around Paris, but also for fun weekends away from the capital, in Ibiza, Saint-Tropez or Île de Ré. Chicer shoppers buy them at Bon Marché, while savvier ones find the hats in their 20th Arrondissement where nobody else goes. **Ecua-Andino Hats** [14 rue Saint-Blaise, 20th] is an insider's destination full of panamas of every color. Traditional, colorful, bright, artistic and *extra fino,* Montecristi hats are reasonably priced since they supply big stores. Come at the beginning of the season to find the greatest variety of choice.

Gambetta's Vintage Shopping

290

Designer bags and shoes, antique frames, chandeliers straight out of grandma's attic... To find great items and get real bargains, the Gambetta area's yard sale is my favorite. This is actually where high-end secondhand shops from posher neighborhoods come to hunt before reselling the gems at higher prices. Far from the boho or hip neighborhoods, you'll find real treasures if you're willing to take the time to search. These sales often take place in May, so keep an eye on their dates while you're in Paris because it's a must! Get off at Gambetta Metro and make your way through this remarkable destination in the arrondissement [Place Gambetta, 20th].

Abribus Couscous

291 Local gathering spot **L'Abribus Café** [56 rue de Bagnolet, 20th] is at the intersection of rue de Fontarabie and rue de la Réunion. Try their excellent couscous; it just so happens to be where Robert Redford likes to go and eat away from prying eyes when he comes to Paris. I love the eclectic vintage decor, folk music on the stereo, Van Morrison, Bill Withers and the low prices. Dishes on their menu go for under €10, so it's a real find.

Place Martin Nadaud

292 Place Martin Nadaud is a small triangular square at the corner of avenue Gambetta and rue de la Bidassoa, just outside the walls of the Père Lachaise Cemetery. Settle in on the sunny terrace of café **Les Foudres** [4 Place Martin Nadaud, 20th] with its nearby cobblestone streets that impart and old country feel. Now, relax! In the Père Lahcaise Cemetery lie the graves of Marcel Proust, Jim Morrison, Oscar Wilde, Molière... Breate, you are amoung friends.

PARIS COUNTRYSIDE

Explore the flower-filled park and medieval
atmosphere at Vincennes, walk through a private
Renaissance-era castle, sleep in a 12th-century abbey,
follow Chateaubriand's footsteps, canoe on Canal des
Amoureux and eat with collectors at the flea market
of Puces de Saint-Ouen.

Paris Countryside

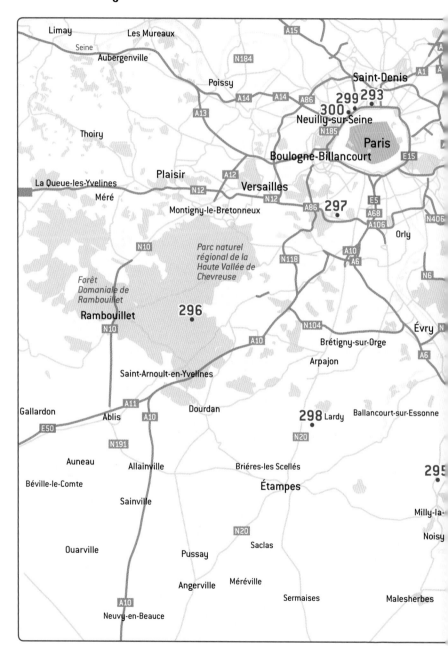

293A

Saint-Ouen Flea Market

293 Lovers of art and vintage finds, knowledgeable antique collectors and curio hunters should not miss out on the flea market **Puces de Saint-Ouen** [142 rue des Rosiers, Saint-Ouen]. It's one of the most famous markets for art and antiques in the world. Flea markets have been transformed in the last few years and the flea marketer profession has become quite hip. Stalls are being updated and contemporary art has made a name for itself alongside hard-to-find antiques. The crowd has become younger and gastronomy lures gourmets in the know. Set aside a whole day to take in this place's unique atmosphere. **Ma Cocotte** (A) [106 rue des Rosiers, Saint-Ouen] restaurant designed by Philippe Starck to be "a house rather than a canteen" is a must. It's the most design-centric and sought-after restaurant here, especially for Sunday brunch.

Sonnenkönig is a festive summer terrace in the heart of the market where you can enjoy homemade burgers, sausages and craft beer set to the sounds of DJ music. **Untilthen** [77 rue des Rosiers, Saint-Ouen] is a high-end contemporary art and emerging artist space founded by three passionate gallery owners. If you like jazz, you absolutely need to stop in at the manouche jazz temple, **La Chope des Puces** [122 rue des Rosiers, Saint-Ouen]. Let's not forget the **MOB** hotel with 350 rooms that has an outdoor cinema, meditation area and an organic vegetarian restaurant to please the hotel world's environmentally responsible golden youth. Take the Metro line 4 to Porte de Clingnancourt station to get there.

294

Medieval Paris at Vincennes

294 There's a medieval architectural treasure at the very end of Metro line 1, at Château de Vincennes station. **Château de Vincennes** [avenue de Paris] was the French monarchy's home until 1682 when Louis XIV decided he preferred Versailles. While you're there, check out the glass roof of **Sainte-Chapelle**, built in 1379, and explore the bulwarks, moats and dungeon. The gardens surrounding the castle have ponds, flowers, bonsais, medicinal plants and a very pretty fragrant garden. Vincennes is also a lovely community with an authentic village vibe. Visit Église Saint-Louis [23 rue Céline Robert] for its Byzantine-inspired architecture, and walk down the town's most commercial street, **rue du Midi**. Right by City Hall and its green square, you'll find **Café de la Mairie**'s terrace [1 rue du Midi]. It's the perfect place to soak up the Vincennes spirit

A Still-Inhabited Romantic Castle

295 Forty-seven kilometers (29 miles) south of Paris, in the Essonne department, you'll find **Château de Courances** [15 rue du Château, Courances]. Registered as a historical monument in 1983, this Renaissance-era private castle was occupied during World War II and used to store German ammunition. It was subsequently abandoned for about 10 years; a tree even had time to grow through a few floors in one of the towers! The castle is now home to the De Ganay family, and you can only visit half of the gigantic space (the castle is actually closed in July and August for family reasons). With 14 water sources, tree-lined walkways, a harmonious mix of plants and stones, moats and small canals, the park is absolutely gorgeous and thought of as one of France's most beautiful, earning it official atatus as a "jardin remarquable" (remakable garden). If you're driving there, take exit No. 13 Milly-la-Forêt on Highway A6, and follow signs to "Courances," which is 5 kilometers (3 miles) away. The castle is not directly accessible by public transit, but you can get there by taking the RER D line and grabbing a taxi at de Boutigny train station for the 14-kilometer (8.7-mile) ride.

295

Sleeping in a 12th-Century Abbey

296

If you're looking to recharge your batteries, here's a beautiful abbey 40 kilometers (30 miles) from Paris. **Abbaye des Vaux de Cernay** [Route d'Auffargis, Cernay-la-Ville] is a 12th-century monastery—once inhabited by monks—that has been turned into a luxury hotel. It's open to the public for visitors looking to spend a day in the abbey's ruins, complete with impressive Gothic vaults. Enjoy the lovely tranquil pond that is home to frolicking geese. You can also stay overnight and reserve a table for a gourmet meal. It's a mystical, chic and very romantic abbey that's accessible by the Baladobus that leaves from the Rambouillet and Saint-Rémy-lès-Chevreuse train stations.

297

Following in Chateaubriand's Footsteps

297 Lovers of literature, history and unique places should go for an interesting visit to the home of Chateaubriand who lived here from 1807 to 1818. The **Vallée-aux Loups** estate [102 rue de Chateaubriand, Châtenay-Malabry] has a museum and is protected as a historical monument. Take a look at where the writer and political figure wrote many of his works. Afterward, wander around the amazing garden full of majestic trees, including some rare species. "I know them all by name, as if they were my children. They're my family, I don't have another," Chateaubriand wrote about his trees in *Mémoires d'Outre-Tombe*. Signs with quotes from the author line the walkway that leads to the house, and there's a lovely café and terrace where you can continue to enjoy the surroundings. The estate is only 30 minutes from Paris by car or you can take the RER B line to Robinson station (terminus) and follow the mapped route that takes 20 to 25 minutes on foot.

Canoeing Down Canal des Amoureux

298 You can catch free concerts in the wonderful **Domaine de Chamarande** [38 rue du Commandant Maurice Arnoux, Chamarande] garden every Sunday in June and July. This place is a beautifully preserved, unknown gem and the perfect place for a breath of fresh air just a few miles outside of Paris. Pack a picnic and enjoy it on the huge lawn that stretches all the way to the foot of the castle. It's the largest public garden in all of Essonne (98 hectares/242 acres) and has earned a "jardin remarquable" (remarkable Garden) label. Combine your visit with a nature walk, as there are many nearby trails, or canoe down **Canal des Amoureux** open as of May 28, from 2 p.m. to 7 p.m. The estate also has animals, which kids love. It's free and easily accessible, since the RER C line (Chamarande station) is 200 meters (655 feet) away.

298

Le Club du Poisson

Eat Beneath a Dinosaur on Île de la Jatte

299

Café La Jatte [60 boulevard Vital Bouhot, Neuilly-sur-Seine] on Île de la Jatte is a historic restaurant where you can eat delicious Italian food beneath a the (fake) skeleton of an aquatic dinosaur hanging from the ceiling. The legendary destination has a wonderful summertime terrace. Take this opportunity to wander around the area and explore the island made famous by 19th-century Impressionist painters, including Van Gogh and Monet. I suggest stopping in at the **Le Petit Poucet** [4 Rond-Point Claude Monet, Levallois-Perret] restaurant by the water. Then walk down boulevard de Levallois Prolongé, where you'll see Neuilly's most beautiful private villas. In the very middle of the island, you'll find a pretty hidden garden with beehives. On the other side of the island, there's a romantic square and picnic area right by the Seine. It's quiet, delightfully peaceful and a good place to spot many species of birds. To get there, take the Metro line 3 to Pont de Levallois station, then take the stairs from the bridge or from Passerelle de la Jatte.

Neuilly's Soul

300

Get off at Porte Maillot on the Metro line 1: You'll be near the Arc de Triomphe, but on the other side of the beltway surrounded by an elegant family neighborhood with a chic village vibe that's unique to Neuilly. I love **Marché des Sablons**, which is open year-round at Place du Marché, from 7:30 a.m. to 1:30 p.m. from Wednesday to Friday, and 7:30 a.m. to 2 p.m. on Sunday. Grab some Moroccan couscous to go, and stock up on spices and fresh produce. Neuilly's epicenter is full of cute clothing and accessory shops. The streets are quiet and will put you at ease. For great Japanese food on a quiet terrace, go to **Orient Extrême** [2 Place Parmentier, Neuilly-sur-Seine]. You might run into members of the Clarins family who have a new office next door. **Michelis Primeurs** [21 rue Madeleine Michelis, Neuilly-sur-Seine] is one of the best fruit stores that always has really fresh produce. **Fafa** [No. 26] is an excellent takeout Asian caterer right across the street. To make like Neuilly's residents, eat at **Livio** [6 rue de Longchamp, Neuilly-sur-Seine], a legendary Italian restaurant patronized by golden youth and high-ranking politicians. The staff, was truly shaken up when owners Pierre Innocenti and his cousin here Stéphane Albertini, were killed in the 2015 Paris terrorist attacks.

Index

The numbers in the Index refer to the Reasons to Love Paris.

"I Love You" wall, 273
404, 50
52, 202
6 Paul Bert, 232

Abbaye des Vaux de
  Cernay, 296
Acne Studios, 94, 125
After the Rain, 8
Aigle, 103
Aki Boulanger, 46
Alléosse, 250
Allison, 104
Amici Miei, 231
Angelina, 97
Apicius, 188
Apple Store, 20
Arènes de Lutèce, 81
Artazart, 206
Astier de Villatte, 16
Au Bain Marie, 143
Au Passage, 235
Au Rocher de Cancale, 24
Aux Bons Fromages, 176
Aux Deux Amis, 220
Aux Merveilleux de Fred,
  246
Ave Maria, 224

Baguett's Café, 42
Ballroom and Beef Club,
  192
Bar du Marché, 104
Bar Ourcq, 274
Baretto di Edgar, 35
Barthélémy, 140
Basilique Notre-Dame-des-
  Victoires, 4
Bassin de l'Arsenal, 212
Bateau ivre, 96
Beau Bien, 59

Beaugrenelle, 145
Benedict, 68
Bibliothèque Mazarine, 109
Bien l'Épicerie, 53
Bistro Volnay, 6
Bistrot Vivienne, 43
Blueberry, 115
Bobbi Brown, 60
Bong, 147
Bonjour Vietnam, 276
Bonjour Vietnam, 80
Bontemps, 58
Bonthés & Bio, 256
Boucherie de la Tour, 176
Boucheron, 1
Boulangerie Véronique
  Mauclerc, 280
Boutique Guerlain, 168
Boutique Maille, 153
Bread & Roses, 149
Breizh Café, 79
Brigitte, 245
Broken Arm, 57
Buddha-Bar-Hotel, 155
Butte Bergeyre, 281
Buvette, 191
By Terry, 21

C'Juice, 94
Café Branly, 131
Café Cassette, 100
Café Charbon, 223
Café Charlot, 58
Café de Flore, 94, 112, 113
Café de l'Homme, 181
Café de la Mairie, 294
Café des 2 Moulins, 268
Café Jacquemart-André, 164
Café Kousmichoff, 169
Café La Jatte, 299
Café Laurent, 102

Café Marlette, 193
Café Marly, 19
Café Pinson, 57
Café Pouchkine, 112
Café Saint Médard, 80
Café Soufflot, 87
Caffè Stern, 27
Canal des Amoureux, 298
Candelaria, 49
Cannibale Café, 218
Canopée, 48
Carette, 181
Carl Marletti, 80
Carrousel du Louvre, 20
Castel, 99
Caulaincourt Square Hostel,
  259
Causses, 196
Caviar Kaspia, 248
Céline, 43, 94
Cevicheria, 25
Chambelland, 224
Champ-de-Mars, 142
Chanel, 60
Chantal Thomass, 26
Chapelle Royale, 139
Château de Courances, 295
Château de Vincennes, 294
Chez Bartolo, 99
Chez Gladines, 93
Chez Janou, 77
Chez Julien, 67
Chez Justine, 223
Chez Léon, 249
Chez Mamane, 93
Chez Omar, 58
Chez Prune, 206
Christian Louboutin, 21
Ciné 13 Théâtre, 257
Cité de la Mode et du
  Design, 84

City Hall Library, 66
Clamato, 226
Claus, 21
Clos Montmartre, 254
CO, 261
Coco Chanel's apartment, 2
Coffee Parisien, 99
Coinstot Vino, 27
Cojean, 145
Colette, 13
Colonne Vendôme, 1
Comédie-Française, 17
Comme des Garçons
   Parfums, 5
Comme des Garçons, 1
Comme des Poissons, 180
Compagnie des Vins
   Surnaturels, 192
Compas, 24
Coulée Verte René-Dumont,
   241
Coutume Instituutti, 134
Coutume, 134
Crazy Horse, 167
Cream, 282
Creed, 125
Cuiller, 266

Da Vito, 225
Dada, 250
David Mallett, 39, 125
Davoli, 135
De Clercq, Les Rois de la
   Frite, 87
Debeaulieu, 190
Déli-Cieux, 198
Derrière, 50
Diptyque, 60
Domaine de Charamande,
   298
Dong Huong, 216
Dose, 80
Du Pain et Des Idées, 206

École Occidentale de
   Méditation, 123
Ecua-Andino Hats, 289
Église Saint-Eustache, 4
Église Saint-Ferdinand-des-
   Ternes, 250

Église Saint-Jean-Baptiste
   de Belleville, 276
Église Saint-Louis, 294
Église Saint-Roch, 4
Église Saint-Sulpice, 98
Electronic DJ Twins, 283
Éléphant Paname, 6
Élysée, 125
Épicerie Générale, 126
Escaliers du Sacré-Cœur,
   269
Espace Pierre Cardin, 158
Etna, 107
Experimental Cocktail Club,
   31, 192

Fafa, 300
Famille Mary, 135
Fée Nature, 37
Fendi, 60
Ferdi, 9
Fine l'Épicerie, 285
Fish Club, 25
Floyd's, 202
Fondation Cartier, 122
Fontaine de Varsovie, 179
Fontaine Médicis, 97
Fontaine Molière, 40
Foyer de la Madeleine, 149
Freddy's, 107
Free'P'Star, 61
Frenchie to Go, 33
Frenchie Wine Bar, 33
Frenchie, 33
FrenchTrotters, 51
Fuxia, 5

Galerie Colbert, 43
Galerie de la Madeleine,
   149
Galerie Kamel Mennour,
   101
Galerie Vivienne, 43
Galignani bookshop, 14
Galleria, 184
Gambetta Shopping, 290
Garde-Robe, 22
George V, 165
Georges, 72
Germain Paradisio, 104

Germain, 104
Gibert Jeune, 89, 123
Gibert Joseph, 123
Givenchy, 60
Grand Cœur, 71
Grand Pigalle Hôtel, 192
Grande Mosquée, 82
Grazie, 53
Grom, 104
Guerlain, 60
Gustave Moreau's House,
   199

Halle Saint Pierre, 272
Hand, 40
Hibou, 116
Holy Bol, 197
Hope Café, 258
Hôtel Amour, 191, 203
Hôtel Bachaumont, 29
Hôtel Bedford, 154
Hôtel Bourg Tibourg, 63
Hôtel Charlemagne, 41
Hôtel Chopin, 197
Hôtel Costes, 7
Hôtel d'Aubusson, 102
Hôtel d'Évreux, 1
Hôtel de l'Abbaye, 100
Hôtel de Vendôme, 1
Hôtel du Nord, 206
Hôtel Edgar, 35
Hôtel Grand Amour, 203
Hôtel Heidelbach, 187
Hôtel Hospitel, 74
Hôtel L'Empire, 22
Hôtel La Perle, 99
Hôtel Particulier, 257
Hôtel Providence, 209
Hôtel Raphael, 170
Hôtel Saint James Albany, 8
Hôtel Thoumieux, 136
Hôtel-Dieu, 74
Huygens, 60

Il Brigante, 255
Il Était Une Fois, 100
Il Posto, 276
Île de la Jatte, 299
India Mahdavi's Showroom,
   128

Institut de Bonté, 210

Jardin des Plantes, 83
Jardin du Moulin-de-la-
    Pointe, 91
Jardin du Palais-Royal, 18
Jardins des Rosiers, 62
Jardins du Trocadéro, 179
Jeanne B, 268
Jeusselin, 135
Jo Malone, 60
Jugestudo, 114
Juice It, 41

KB Caféshop, 193
Kenzo, 41
Kiehl's, 60
Kiez, 260
Kigawa, 118
Kilian, 2
Kilo Shop, 61
Kinugawa, 162
Klay, 38
Kotteri Ramen Naritake, 44
Kunitoraya, 45
Kusmi, 169
Kyobashi, 222

L'Abribus Café, 291
L'Ami Jean, 137
L'Arbre à Lettres, 242
L'Arc, 172
L'As du Fallafel, 62
L'Assiette, 118
L'Avant Comptoir de la Mer,
    107
L'Avant Comptoir, 107
L'Ébauchoir, 240
L'Ébouillanté, 67
L'Écailler du bistrot, 232
L'Éclair, 135
L'Écume des Pages, 113
L'Endroit, 247
L'Hôtel, 111
L'Oasis d'Aboukir, 34
L'Occitane, 60
L'Orangerie, 188
La Baraque A., 211
La Botte Gardiane, 228
La Cave du Moulin Vieux, 93

La Cave, 232
La Cerise sur le Chapeau,
    100
La Chambre aux Confitures,
    193
La Cocotte, 232
La Ferme d'Hugo, 173
La Fidélité, 204
La Flèche d'Or, 286
La Hune, 94
La Mangerie, 70
La Mangerie, 99
La Marée Jeanne, 25
La Palette, 105
La Petite Halle, 277
La Piñata, 200
La REcyclerie, 262
La Réserve, 158
La Rotonde, 274
La Salle-à-Manger, 52
La Splendens Factory, 253
La Trinquette, 50
Lancôme, 157
Lanqi-Spa, 141
Lao Lane Xang 2, 90
Lapérousse, 110
Laurent, 158
Le 11ème Domaine, 219
Le 68, 168
Le Bar, 111
Le Barav, 57
Le Baron Rouge, 239
Le Basilic, 127
Le Baudelaire, 3
Le Bistrot Paul Bert, 232
Le Bon Georges, 194
Le Bon Marché, 124
Le Bristol, 188
Le Burgundy, 3
Le Café qui Parle, 268
Le Chat Noir, 252
Le Comptoir Général, 208,
    283
Le Coupe-Chou, 87
Le Crabe Marteau, 251
Le Dalí, 10
Le Fanfaron, 230
Le Flandrin, 188
Le Fumoir, 15
Le Grand Colbert, 43

Le Grand Restaurant, 188
Le Griffonnier, 125
Le Kiosque des
    Noctambules, 17
Le Merle Moqueur, 93
Le Meurice, 10
Le Napoléon, 201
Le Pain Quotidien, 5, 18
Le Perchoir, 214
Le Petit Oiseau Va Sortir,
    227
Le Petit Poucet, 299
Le Petit Rétro, 173
Le Progrès, 58
Le Restaurant, 111
Le Salon des Miroirs, 197
Le Syndicat, 202
Le Victoria, 154
Le Village, 152
Le Vin de Bellechasse, 130
Legrand Filles & Fils, 43
Leoni's Deli, 37
Les 400 Coups, 244
Les Bijoux de Nico, 93
Les Cailloux, 93
Les Chouettes, 57
Les Cocottes, 132
Les Deux Magots, 112
Les Douches, 200
Les Éditeurs, 116
Les Foudres, 292
Les Gourmets des Ternes,
    248
Les Jardins du Marais, 234
Les Ombres, 131
Les P'tites Indécises, 219
Les Perchés du Chai, 265
Les Piaules, 221
Levalet, 275
Lipp, 94
Little Cantine, 87
Little Italy, 24
Little Japan, 44
Livio, 300
LO / A, 59
Luisa Maria, 116

M. O. B., 84
Ma Cocotte, 293
Mac, 60

Maison Blanche, 163, 188
Maison de la Chantilly, 135
Maison Desgranges, 174
Maison Hermès, 150
Maison Internationale, 120
Maison Margiela, 94
Maison Plisson, 53
Maison Pou, 250
Mama Shelter, 286
Mamie Burger, 201
Mangiamo Italiano, 54
Manko, 163
Marc Jacobs, 5
Marcel, 257
Marché aux Fleurs, 149
Marché Bio Raspail, 95
Marché Biologique des
    Batignolles, 247
Marché Couvert de Passy,
    174
Marché de Belleville, 288
Marché de La Bastille, 217
Marché des Enfants Rouges,
    54
Marché des Sablons, 300
Mariage Frères, 20
Marin d'Eau Douce, 274
Market, 161
Marlon, 133
Mathis, 160, 192
Mems, 207
Merci, 53
Métro Château d'Eau, 201
Michelis Primeurs, 300
MIJE Fourcy, 67
Miznon, 62
Mme Shawn, 57
Mmmozza, 54
MOB, 293
Moncoeur Belleville, 284
Monsieur Bleu, 182
Montaigne Market, 166
Moonshiner, 225
Motsch, 248
Moulin de la Galette, 257
Mouzaïa, 278
Musée d'Ennery, 171
Musée de Cluny, 85
Musée de l'Orangerie, 11
Musée de la Môme, 215

Musée de Montmartre, 254
Musée des Arts décoratifs,
    12
Musée des arts et métiers,
    55
Musée du Luxembourg, 97
Musée du Quai Branly, 131
Musée Guimet, 187
Musée Jacquemart-André,
    164
Musée Picasso, 64
Musée Rodin, 129
Muséum National d'Histoire
    Naturelle, 83
My favorite stroll, 159

Nanashi, 57
Nathalie Dumeix, 243
Night Flight, 29
Nils Avril, 224
Nina, 118
No Stress Café, 191
Noglu, 27
Nomad's, 5
Nord Marais, 59
Nose, 28
Notre-Dame-de-
    l'Assomption, 4
Nüba, 84, 283

Ob-La-Di, 49
Ober Mamma, 213
Odette Paris, 88
Oh My Cream!, 106
Openspace, 229
Orient Extrême, 300
Oroyona, 80

Palais de Chaillot, 179
Palais de Tokyo, 182
Palais du Luxembourg, 97
Palais Galliera, 184
Panthéon Bouddhique, 187
Panthéon, 87
Parc André-Citroën, 148
Parc de la Cité
    Internationale
    Universitaire, 120
Parc des Buttes-Chaumont,
    276

Parc Georges-Brassens, 146
Parc Kellermann, 91
Paris Féni, 224
Paris Jazz Corner, 81
Paris New York, 201
Paris-London, 149
Passage du Caire, 32
Passage du Chantier, 242
Passage du Grand-Cerf, 24
Passage Jouffroy, 197
Passage Molière, 76
Passage Verdeau, 197
Passy Plaza, 174
Pâtisserie des Rêves, 178
Paul, 11
Pavillon de la Fontaine, 97
Pavillon des Canaux, 274
Pavillon des Lettres, 156
Péniche Antipode, 274
Petit Cler, 135
PH7 Équilibre, 195
Philharmonie, 279
Phô 18, 90
Pierre Frey, 29
Pizza Chic, 100
Place Colette, 17
Place Dalida, 257
Place Dauphine, 23
Place de la Contrescarpe,
    80
Place de la Madeleine, 149
Place des Abbesses, 267
Place des Victoires, 41
Place des Vosges, 65
Place du Marché Saint-
    Honoré, 5
Place Louis Aragon, 75
Place Paul Verlaine, 93
Place Saint-Georges, 194
PNY (Paris New York), 57
Polidor, 116
Pollen, 276
Pont de Bir-Hakeim, 144
Pont Neuf, 23
Popelini, 193
Première Pression
    Provence, 193
Prescription Cocktail Club,
    192
Printemps, 198

Puces de Saint-Ouen, 293
Puces de Vanves, 121
Pulcinella, 263

Quai and Gare d'Austerlitz, 84
Quartier des Batignolles, 247

Rachel's sur le Canal, 206
Rachel's, 68
Racines 2, 22
Ralph's, 108
Rasa Yoga, 86
Raviolis Chinois Nord-Est, 287
Résine, 276
Restaurant Champeaux, 48
Restaurant de l'Hôtel Bachaumont, 192
Restaurant du Park Hyatt, 1
Rosa Bonheur, 138
Rosa Bonheur, 276
Rose Bakery, 193
Rose Bunker, 270
Rue Crémieux, 237
Rue de Lévis, 245
Rue du Faubourg Saint-Antoine, 242
Rue du Faubourg Saint-Denis, 202
Rue du Midi, 294
Rue Lepic, 268
Rue Sainte-Marthe, 200

Sainte-Chapelle, 294
Salon Coiff1rst, 157
Salsamenteria di Parma, 194
Sapporo, 44
Schou, 171
Season, 57
Septime La Cave, 226
Septime, 226
Serres d'Auteuil, 186
Seymour +, 200
Shangri-La Hotel, 183
Shu, 117
Silencio, 36
Sinople, 38

SŌMA, 49
Sonnenkönig, 293
Sourire de Saigon, 264
Soya, 238
Square Caulaincourt, 259
Square Colbert, 233
Square des Batignolles, 247
Square du Temple, 56
Square du Vert-Galant, 24
Square Louis XVI, 151
Square Montsouris, 119
Square René Viviani-Montebello, 89
Square Saint-Gilles Grand Veneur, 78
Stock Claudie Pierlot, 207
Stock Les Petites, 207
Stock Maje, 207
Stock Sandro, 73
Stock Zadig & Voltaire, 73
Stocks Azzedine Alaïa, 73
Stocks Gerard Darel, 30
Stohrer, 24
Street Art 13 project, 92
Studio Pilates 16, 178

Taeko, 54
Taschen, 104
Télescope, 47
Terra Corsa, 193
Terrass' Hôtel, 271
Terroirs d'Avenir, 33
Thaddaeus Ropac, 283
The Asado Club, 283
The Bottle Shop, 236
Thé Cool, 175
Théâtre des Champs-Élysées, 163
Theatrum Botanicum, 122
Tigre Yoga Club, 185
Très Honoré, 5
Tribeca, 135
Trois Fois Plus de Piment, 69
Tui Na, 141
Tuileries, 11

Udon Bistro Kunitoraya, 45
Uma, 5
Une Maille à l'Endroit, 177

Untilthen, 293
Urfa Dürüm, 202

Vallée-aux-Loups Estate, 297
Van Cleef & Arpels, 1
Velan, 205
Victoria 1836, 172
Villa Léandre, 257
Villa Passy, 174
Village Café, 245

Wait, 59
Water-Bar, 13

Yohji Yamamoto, 41
Yoom, 193
You Decide, 173
Yoyo, 182

ZA, 48
Zo, 156

Acknowledgments

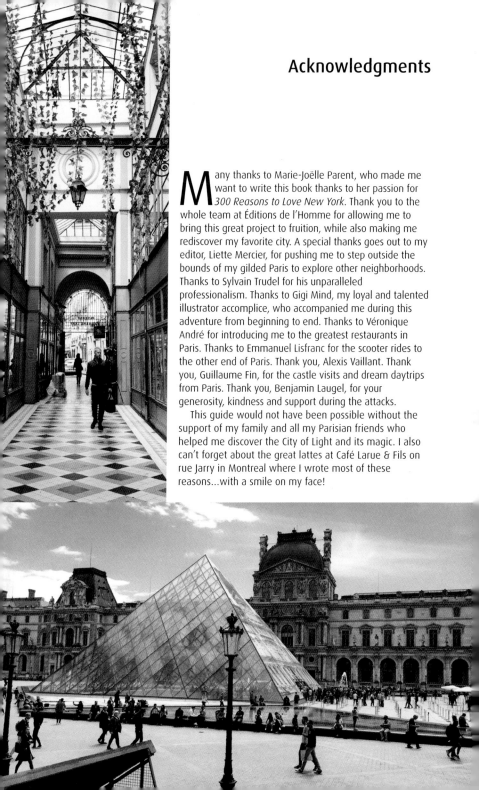

Many thanks to Marie-Joëlle Parent, who made me want to write this book thanks to her passion for *300 Reasons to Love New York*. Thank you to the whole team at Éditions de l'Homme for allowing me to bring this great project to fruition, while also making me rediscover my favorite city. A special thanks goes out to my editor, Liette Mercier, for pushing me to step outside the bounds of my gilded Paris to explore other neighborhoods. Thanks to Sylvain Trudel for his unparalleled professionalism. Thanks to Gigi Mind, my loyal and talented illustrator accomplice, who accompanied me during this adventure from beginning to end. Thanks to Véronique André for introducing me to the greatest restaurants in Paris. Thanks to Emmanuel Lisfranc for the scooter rides to the other end of Paris. Thank you, Alexis Vaillant. Thank you, Guillaume Fin, for the castle visits and dream daytrips from Paris. Thank you, Benjamin Laugel, for your generosity, kindness and support during the attacks.

This guide would not have been possible without the support of my family and all my Parisian friends who helped me discover the City of Light and its magic. I also can't forget about the great lattes at Café Larue & Fils on rue Jarry in Montreal where I wrote most of these reasons...with a smile on my face!